By Hook or By Cook

The Official Nevada Brothel Cookbook

Cat House Cuisine Concocted
by Nevada's Finest Working Ladies

Edited by J.R. Schwartz

*"Tell me what you eat, and I will
tell you what you are."*

— Brillat-Savarin

*"Bang-whang-whang goes the drum,
and tootle-te tootle the fife,
There is no keeping one's haunches still,
It's the greatest pleasure in life."*

— Robert Browning

*"She gave me a smile
I could feel in my hip pocket."*

— Raymond Chandler

"There is no such thing as bad sex."

— Anonymous

ACKNOWLEDGEMENTS

Several good people helped to put this book together, and I am grateful for all their assistance, suggestions, recommendations and creative contributions they made.

The list is long, but what the hell, special thanks go out to: Tinka, Evelyn Phillips, Larry Bettis, John Sieckert, Tom & Lucy Hickey, Madam Sheri Hodge, Kathy Winterton, Arnie Gonzales, Geoff Bushell, Brad Nottingham, David Heimbach, Sunny Hodge, Karyn Williams, Pug Ostling, Jim Hodge, Greg Greenlee, Rod Allen, T. Rice, Karen Rupkey, George Nicol, Darcy Williamson, Mark Flory, my sister Nicki Troutman, Lyn Stallard, Margie Goltz, T.S., Jill De Olivera, Ron Lube, Jim Houghton, Diane Cooper, Sue Gibson, Damon Knight for extraordinary editorial insight, and as always, Jeffrey Huber.

This book is dedicated to Norma and Allan,

who knew how to cook too.

DISCLAIMER

Alright, we all like to eat, and have great sex. In fact, if you've read the Quotes page you know there's no such thing as bad sex (sort of like there's no such thing as *"bad breath"* when you consider the alternative).

But there is such a thing as over eating, and not chewing your food before swallowing.

So, beware, this book does not discuss calories, cholesterol, or what happens if you're out of shape and do things that are detrimental to your health.

Try to use good judgment in the quantities of food, calories and pleasure you consume and expend. And don't forget to drink plenty of water and other nutritious substances in your daily regimen.

Other than that, try to have a healthy and happy time, follow the advice and direction of positive roll models, and don't be thinking about suing us if you eat or drink too much.

Finally, names and characters in this cookbook are the products of my imagination. However, the recipes themselves are entirely edible. Beyond that, any resemblance to persons, living or deceased, are entirely coincidental.

Regards and Enjoy,

INTRODUCTION

Welcome to the cookbook that's going to put a smile on your face and food in your stomach. Full bodied menus that are guaranteed to bring you the ultimate epicurean enjoyment. Recipes from some of the finest courtesans and hookers to ever work Nevada's most unique pleasure realms.

These ladies specialize in satisfying physical and sexual appetites, and along the way they give a whole new meaning to such phrases as *"bone appetit"* and *"feel like eating something?"*

But their restaurants are sexual palaces too, where *Wok on the Wild Side* becomes more than rice and fortune cookies, and recipes for *Whipped Cream Experience, The Binaca Blast* or *Crabs Like Never Before* can conjure up fascinating images of an indulgent time to be well spent without indigestion or a lot of calories to follow. *By Hook or by Cook*, these ladies get the job done nicely.

This is creative cat house cuisine at its finest. Included here are sixty-nine incredible recipes to blow your mind (perhaps something else too, along the way), with insights by some of Nevada's finest ladies of the night. Tasty and suggestive possibilities that you can share with your favorite partner. If the way to the bedroom is through the kitchen, these recipes should help guide you down the path better than any road map possibly could.

Perhaps you're new to the concept of legal prostitution in Nevada. If so, here are some thoughts for you to digest. The state of Nevada has allowed legal prostitution to exist in communities of less than 200,000 people since 1967, when the Storey County Commissioners legalized and licensed the first lawful brothel in Nevada: the Mustang Ranch.

Now, almost thirty years later, thirty-four legally licensed cat houses are in business throughout the state. From the outskirts of Reno and Carson City, east along Interstate 80 into towns like Carlin, Winnemucca, Elko and Wells, then south to Ely, Beatty and Pahrump (the locals call it *"Pay rump"*), to just outside the bright night lights of Las Vegas, you'll find these pleasure points with names appealing to prurient visions of self-indulgent delights: The Cherry Patch, Mabel's Whorehouse, The New Sagebrush Red Light Ranch, P.J's Lucky Strike, The Stardust Gentleman's Club, along with more than two dozen others.

Women of every persuasion work these cat houses, offering pleasurable possibilities too numerous to mention. What they have in mind for you might be a Whipped Cream Experience, The Binaca Blast or Crabs Like Never Before.

With all their uninhibited free spiritedness, it's only natural that these ladies would concoct some outrageous recipes in their spare time guaranteed to elicit several responses from more than the kitchen. One lady mentioned that, "In deviation there are dynamics." Another said, "In these cat houses bad is good, but naughty is nicer."

These women come to the kitchen with sweet, mystical ingredients: Ambrosia, nectar from the gods, creative potions and combinations delicately whipped into mouth-watering experiences. From Texas-sized to finger-licking good. Bodacious treats, sometimes creamed, sometimes wilted. Erotic imagery and love potions designed to induce ecstasy, to inspire, enhance and allure. Courtesans blending their ingredients and talents with soft sounds and essences, gently tipping the scales of desire.

It has been suggested in fabled lore that certain fragrances are powerful turn-ons that can help alleviate sexual maladies and certain *"indiscretions."* And, we're not just talking pumpkin pie and doughnuts from the kitchen here. *"Lavender and musk, arouse from the dusk."*

Just as the wisdom of the Kama Sutra written one thousand years ago guided people towards the enhancement of pleasure, **By Hook or By Cook, The Official Brothel Cookbook of Nevada** today offers you enjoyable epicurean adventures that can take you beyond your kitchen and help further your pursuits.

These ladies can cook too! With diverse talents and attributes rivaling those of Julia Childs and the stars of *"New Wave Hookers 4,"* they're here to offer you savory rewards for your cooking efforts that will take you far beyond your talents in the kitchen.

TABLE OF CONTENTS

APPETEASERS

BREAKFAST IN BED

SOUPS & SALADS

DINNERS

DESSERTS

AROMA THERAPY

APPENDIX

ORDER FORM

Appeteasers

LORENA BOBBIT'S BEENIE WEENIES

A madam whose brothel brought cheers
had patrons past due in arrears.
So she threatened to sue,
for payments past due,
or cut off their peckers with shears.

Many hookers have been heard evoking a Lorena Bobbitt thought when sales are slow in the cat houses: *"Use it or lose it."*

This appeteaser has definite sexual implications, and is more than just a conversation piece as an *hors d'oeuvre.* The mere mention of Lorena's name can send grown men into shock, especially when you tell them that this recipe serves 1 to 20 people, depending on how thin you slice the weenies, or how dull the knife is.

However, you might calm nerves (and dangling nerve endings) by mentioning that these weenies have been shaken and cleaned well, with all the dirt and gravel particles removed from the meaty parts.

The beauty of this treat is in the ease of preparation. Just get a can of low sodium pork and beans and a package of low fat, all beef frankfurters, pre-slice your weenies, toss all the ingredients into a pan and bring to a gradual but proper intensity before serving. Then, when you're ready, just dump them onto a plate and offer up plenty of toothpicks.

To add to the festivities you might place a carving knife adjacent to your platter (for perfect slicing and dicing we recommend Chicago Cutlery), and to brighten up the banter and conversation you could mention a couple more of Lorena's favorite recipes that you've recently heard about: *Spaghetti in Pete's Balls* and *Chipped Beef.*

OYSTERS ROCK YER FELLER

Remember the famous governor from New York who supposedly dropped dead while his *"oysters"* were being rocked by his former secretary? Well, this little appeteaser isn't named after him, and it's not exactly what you'd get from Chef Jules Alciatore at Antoines in New Orleans either, but it's real tasty and considered to be an aphrodisiac by many who claim that sexual enhancement and longevity soon follow digestion.

It all depends on who digests what here, so use some imagination and, who knows, you may bop until you drop too with these tasty little nuggets.

A good shopping tip to remember is this: when buying oysters don't get large ones, or those that appear to be opening. Large oysters are difficult to swallow, and have a tendency to gag people, while the partially opened ones are not fresh and will probably make you gag too.

INGREDIENTS

1/2 cup shrimp, crab or lobster
5 tablespoons butter
1/2 of a 10 ounce package of frozen chopped spinach,
     thawed slightly
2 tablespoons minced scallions
1/4 teaspoon salt
1/8 teaspoon cayenne pepper
1/4 cup Anisette or Pernod
1/4 cup soft dried or crushed bread crumbs
1 tablespoon chopped parsley
1 bay leaf, finely crumbled
1 garlic clove, minced
24 small oysters on the half shell
2 slices of bacon, diced
1/2 cup grated Parmesan cheese
   (continued)

Lemon wedges for garnish
Fresh pepper to taste
Rock salt

COOKING INSTRUCTIONS FOR OYSTERS ROCK YER FELLER:

Preheat oven to 425° F. In a one quart sauce pan place melted butter and spinach, with bay leaf, salt and cayenne, stirring occasionally, until the spinach is heated through. Toss in bread crumbs and set aside. In a frying pan, brown your minced garlic, parsley and scallions, then add your top meat of lobster, shrimp or crab meat, continuing to blend your ingredients.

When all are browned add to the spinach and mix well.

Place enough rock salt in a large, shallow baking pan or in pie tins to keep the oysters in the shell from tipping over. Arrange your oysters in the pan and spoon the spinach mixture on top. Sprinkle with bacon and Parmesan cheese. Bake 10 minutes, or until bacon is crisp. Garnish with lemon wedges and serve with tiny forks.

POSSIBLE SUGGESTIONS FOR SERVING ATTIRE:

Oysters Rock Yer Feller sounds upscale, but you can feel comfortable wearing relatively casual early evening attire. To accentuate your legs a spandex body-hugging mini skirt with full zipper front should get the juices flowing nicely.

But, if you're even more into casual, try a Bolero style jacket with fringed back and sleeves, over a lace-up bustier and matching zip back pants with peep-hole grommets. There's nothing like peep holes to excite the deviant expectations of that special person in your life.

In either event, a **Frederick's of Hollywood** catalog should accommodate you nicely. See the reference section in the back of the book for their address and telephone number.

QUICKIES WITH HARD SAUCE

Quickies. That's right. Faster than a positive reaction in a petri dish at the Free Clinic after a bad night of unsafe sex with some not-too-distant relative. We're talking quicker than a New York minute here...not quite superman, but faster than a speeding bullet. You know the allusions: Hair trigger, getting the lead out a little too soon, the train pulling out of the station earlier than scheduled, "real time," immediate, and oops!

Not exactly, *"Was it as good for you as it was for me babe?"*

Quickies. We're talking five minutes or less to prepare. Carrot sticks, celery sticks, radishes, scallions, mushrooms, zucchini wedges, olives and apple slices. Fresh, fun stuff that's immediately edible.

Now, once you've hacked or sliced these little pieces of health foods into serving sized morsels you'll want to place them on a serving platter and then ask your partner if he/she would like to help you prepare the *'Hard Sauce.'* If that question doesn't begin to raise a smile, you could be doing carrot sticks alone this night with a different recipe for hard sauce! Your basic hard sauce is real easy to prepare and it complements any of the appeteasers mentioned above.

INGREDIENTS
1/2 pound of sweet butter, softened
1 cup sugar
1/3 cup rum or brandy
1 teaspoon vanilla extract

Cream the butter and sugar well. Then add your rum or brandy to it, just a few drops at a time, and beat until it is fluffy. Finally beat in the vanilla and chill until you're ready to serve.

You might be drinking some of the alcohol on the side at this point during preparation, with a buzz of expectation, so dress for it. Body language is important here. Be innocent yet extremely provocative because it will soon be time to play.

Perhaps a **Pleasure Points of Nevada** tee shirt and black leather panties, along with strappy patent leather sandals with 4-5″ high heels (the kind Betty Page wore in the early 50s) is appropriate. See the reference section for the **Dream Dresser Catalog.**

TASTES LIKE BALLS

"Balls," said the Queen. "If I had them I'd be king!"

—The Queen of Hearts from *Alice in Wonderland*

Tasty Lacy from P.J.'s Lucky Strike in Elko came up with this recipe for balls. She's a petite brunette with hazel eyes, long, long legs, and is a helluva dancer. She also knows a few things about balls. This first recipe is for Swedish meatballs.

INGREDIENTS FOR SWEDISH MEATBALLS

2 tablespoons butter
3 tablespoons minced onions
3/4 cup fresh bread crumbs
3/4 cup half & half
1/2 pound ground round steak
1/3 pound ground veal
1/3 pound ground pork
1 egg
Salt & pepper to taste
1/2 cup flour
3/4 cup cream

Melt your butter in a large frying pan and saute your onions in it. In a large bowl mix your bread crumbs in the half & half, then add the ground meats, egg, onions, salt and pepper, mixing it well, before shaping the ball into bite-sized nuggets about one inch in diameter, then coat them with the flour. Reserve 1 tablespoon of flour for gravy later.

Next you want to melt some more butter in your frying pan and brown the meatballs over medium heat until they're cooked. Finally, remove them from the pan when cooked, and prepare your gravy by adding the tablespoon of flour to the juices in the pan, along with the 3/4 cup of cream, whisking until it's a smooth consistency, simmering for about five minutes. Pour the gravy over the balls, and serve hot when ready.

OPAL'S
DIP & LICK

Opal is a stone-cold fox who works at the Lazy B Guest Ranch, located a few miles southeast of the town of Fallon. Occasionally she likes to concoct an edible treat and she says this appeteaser is real quick to make, yet uses inexpensive ingredients. You need one eight-ounce wedge of low-fat cream cheese and one pint of marshmallow fluff goop.

Put the cream cheese and marshmallow goop in a blender and turn it on low speed, whipping it into a nice serving consistency. Then place it in your refrigerator to chill until you're ready to serve it to that someone special.

It's perfect for dipping fruits into just as is, but if you want to spice it up (for dipping vegetables) just add some chutney or picante sauce to the top of it and serve with your favorite vegetable slices, or any variety of chips.

Opal is a true philosopher queen with a lot of insight into many of life's sexual facets and oddities. She says, *"Anything dippable is excellent,"* so use some creativity here and feed more than your nymphomania. If you want to learn more about life from Opal she suggests you stop by the Lazy B Guest Ranch. This therapist has a good working philosophy and enjoys her job. She says, *"Anyone can sell sex. I'm here to sell passion and a good time!"*

SUGGESTIONS FOR SERVING ATTIRE

As with any appeteaser, feel comfortable in your attire, but don't be afraid to be defiant and alluring. You want to captivate, fascinate and ultimately gravitate. You want to tantalize and tempt whoever you're playing and eating with.

A Rough Rider jean jacket left open, with a Ladies Erotic Chain Link and Leather Harness underneath will do wonders to tempt the imagination (see the reference for the **Fantasy Island** catalog).

Also, while you're serving up food, get ready to serve up tasty safe sex with *Kiss of Mint* flavored condoms. These condoms, scented with mint accoutrements, may help to provide the protection you want, while also leaving a good taste in your mouth.

For more information about *Kiss of Mint* condoms (and several others), refer to the **Stamford Collection** catalog in the back of this cookbook.

SAVORY MELONS

When I think of savory melons I think of Anna Nicole Smith, Jenna Jameson or some Hagerman farm girl who knows a thing or two about the pleasures of life.

Melons, conjuring up complex thoughts of fruition, cornucopia... the horn of plenty. Concealed yet approachable. Pronounced yet unseen. Ample and bountiful. Casabas... rind bearing, sweet flesh fruits from Asia Minor. Full flavored beauties... from orange fleshed to yellow cuties.

Melons come in pairs, and so do these recipes. One involves balls, the other wedges.

MELON RECIPE #1

INGREDIENTS

2 large canteloupes
1 pint vanilla ice cream, softened
1/4 cup heavy cream, whipped
Fresh mint leaves (from your grocer's produce department)
Fresh berries in season (take your pick)

Cut the canteloupes into halves, remove the seeds and guts, drain and discard. Scoop out the inside of each canteloupe, leaving about 1/4 inch of canteloupe flesh in each shell. Freeze the shells overnight.

You next want to finely chop the scooped out canteloupe fruit and blend it with the pint of vanilla ice cream. Finally, fold in the whipped cream and fresh berries onto the canteloupe and ice cream and place in the canteloupe shells. Refreeze them until you're ready to serve on a hot summer day. Believe me, this will melt in more than just your mouth.

MELON RECIPE #2

INGREDIENTS

1 large canteloupe
1/4 cup sugar
1/2 cup orange juice
2 tablespoons lemon juice
1/2 cup light rum

Cut the canteloupe in half, then cut the fruit into melon ball shapes with a melon ball scooper. Next, in a bowl combine the sugar, orange juice, lemon juice and rum. Pour over melon balls. If any juice and extract is left over ask your guest if he'd like the opportunity to lick the bowl, and then make him work for it. If he wants to taste the pleasures of your "Savory Melons," he should know what he has to do, right?

When Tricky Dick was arrested for felons,
in the slammer he screamed, "Bring me melons!"
They're juicy and warm,
and do me no harm,
To pretend they're boobs in my cell-um.

ROCKY MOUNTAIN OYSTERS

There was a hot girl named Star,
who had sex from near and from far.
When asked to explain,
she replied with disdain,
"I'm trying to buy a new car."

Star is another one of the truly fine ladies to have worked at P.J.'s Lucky Strike in Elko. Part Mayan Indian, part celestial, this tall beauty is quite experienced about balls, those glandular dangular hangers that are the basis of so much orgasmic pleasure. She has an ability to work wonders with them with a confident knowledge that is more than encyclopedic.

Balls. We're talking big beef balls, and humonguous sheep balls. If you've been to the State Fair lately, you know what I'm talking about. Huge danglers. Scrotum encased love lobes. The beginning of the future. Progeny, or an appeteaser, take your pick.

But, whichever ones you decide to use for your recipe just make sure they're fresh. Old smelly balls are a real turn-off, and can put a damper on the ambient expectations to follow.

INGREDIENTS FOR ROCKY MOUNTAIN OYSTERS

2 pounds of your favorite balls (bull or sheep)
3-4 fresh lemons
Worcestershire sauce to taste
1 cup flour
1/2 teaspoon paprika
1/2 teaspoon cayenne pepper
1/2 teaspoon garlic granules (not salt or powder)
Course ground black pepper to taste

From your local meat and sausage market you want to get two pounds of fresh balls, which you will quarter into bite-sized chunks, then briefly marinate in the juice of squeezed lemons.

Next mix your flour with the paprika, cayenne, garlic granules, and black pepper, then dredge your balls in it.

Finally, saute the balls in olive oil over medium heat until they are cooked, then serve hot.

Oysters are an aphrodisiac,
guaranteeing pleasures in the sack.
They'll bring you straight outta your shell,
making you smile while both heads swell.

NUT NIBBLES

Nuts, stones, kernels and cojones. Although relatively contemporary, this treat is originally attributed to the mythological Greek God Testiclees, who is said to have enjoyed nibbled nuts from time to time.

INGREDIENTS

1 pound of shelled nuts (pecans, walnuts or almonds)
2 tablespoons of melted butter

Preheat the oven to 250 degrees. Place the nuts on a baking sheet and pour the butter over them. Toss the nuts with a slotted spoon to coat them well.

Next you'll want to bake them for 10-15 minutes until they're crispy and golden brown. You can shake the pan or stir the nuts to achieve even cooking.

Cool and serve when ready.

It's rumored that John Wayne Bobbitt got a new job.
He's working for Snap-On Tools.

Cowboy's Bubble Bath
(Bean Dip)

"And let them pass, as they will too soon,
with the bean flowers bloom
and the blackbird's tune
and May and June."

—Robert Burns

And catch the essence around the room! Bubble bath. Aroma therapy. Definitely the potential for a one-man Jacuzzi bubbler here. The name of this recipe comes from the results that probably will follow you around the room and depending upon the beans used, will also determine the ambience to follow. The secret is in the beans and how pasty you get them.

We're talking big time aroma therapy bean dip here. Gas, wind and flatulence come with garbanzos, kidneys and pintos.

INGREDIENTS

You'll want to boil approximately one pound of assorted beans (or pick your favorite kind), strain them through a sieve, and place to the side in your kitchen.

Next, into a bowl add:

1/2 cup shredded sharp Cheddar cheese
1 teaspoon garlic salt
2 cloves of finely diced garlic
1 teaspoon chili powder
1/2 teaspoon salt and a dash of cayenne pepper
2 teaspoons vinegar
2 teaspoons Worcestershire sauce
4 slices of bacon, crumbled and diced

Blend all of the ingredients together here and heat them carefully in a sauce pan (or double boiler if you're concerned about scalding your pots). When all is ready, scoop into a bowl and place on a serving tray with corn chips or any other firm dippable that will allow the bean mixture to adhere to.

After eating this dip you'll soon be conjuring and rumbling up thoughts and sounds more appropriate for the Frenchman "Le Petomane," than a walk on the palace grounds with the Queen Mother. The *"French Fartiste"* wasn't exactly known as the perfumed gardener after a stirring round of bean dip, and neither will your buckaroo after eating this stuff, so dress accordingly.

If you're concerned about scorching more than the pots in your kitchen, I recommend crotchless panties for her, and maybe a pair of riding chaps from the **Tom of Finland Catalog** for him.

Now, another nice thing about this treat is that if you want to take a dip after enjoying this appeteaser, and your budget is a little short when it comes to the Jacuzzi/spa (or you don't even have one), even a small sized bathtub will work with both of you in it, and with him providing the bubble machine. No timid souls here, please.

There are many suggestive possibilities here. First and foremost start with scented candles, and perhaps some erotic and sensual jewelry rarely seen in public *(**The Stamford Catalog for Women Collection** is a good place to go hunting).

Also, romantic music should be thoughtfully selected for the enjoyable moments to follow. I don't recommend *"They Call the Wind Mariah," "Dust in the Wind"* or Bob Dylan's *"Blowing in the Wind."*

Mary had a little lamb
you've heard this tale before,
But did you know she passed some gas
and had a little more?

A Randi Delight

"The nakedness of woman is the work of God."

—William Blake

First, let me just say that Randi is one of the most stunningly beautiful women to have ever worked in a cat house, in the world, ever. Dark skinned, with the body of a superstar, and a confidence level projected far beyond this solar system, she is a one-of-a-kind woman of substance. Last seen working at Simone's de Paris in Winnemucca, Randi is absolutely amazing, with an appeteaser to match.

For a taste of simple pleasure try this delight, and then hope to cross Randi's path in your lifetime to further discuss the nuances of her treat. It's a cheese spread and it's real easy to prepare.

INGREDIENTS
6 ounces soft goat cheese (Rollingstone, Chevre or
   something similar)
6 ounces softened cream cheese
1 tablespoon of minced shallot
1/8 cup minced parsley (that's fresh!)
2 tablespoons minced red pepper (fresh from your
   grocer's produce department)
2 cloves minced garlic
1/8 cup minced celery
1/2 teaspoon paprika

Mix all the ingredients thoroughly, shape into a ball, and chill for two hours. Two hours later you'll be ready to serve it. But, for the next two hours, while it's chilling down, you'll have time to heat it up with your partner, right? Randi says to go for it!

A TASTE
OF GINGER

RIDDLE: "What's old and wrinkled and tastes like Ginger?"
ANSWER: "Fred Astaire's nose."

(It's a joke.) Ginger is a tropical herb that has been used as an aphrodisiac and stimulant in the East Indies and China for over 3,000 years. The end result: Excited genitals, firmer erections and lustier sexual desires. If you could only ask Fred he'd probably tell you.

What we have in mind here is a ginger-salsa dip that can help you move into another edible mode, and maybe even into a dance step or two later.

INGREDIENTS

2 pounds ripe red tomatoes
1 tablespoon olive oil
2 teaspoons finely grated fresh ginger
1 teaspoon red wine vinegar
2 tablespoons lemon juice
Cilantro to taste
Yellow or green pepper slices for taste,
 color and texture
Diced pineapple to taste
Green onions, sliced
1 clove garlic, finely chopped
Salt & pepper to taste

You want to dice the tomatoes into 1/4 inch cubes and place them in a bowl. But first, cut out and remove the hard core areas of the tomatoes that you wouldn't ever eat or serve to fancy guests. Then add the remaining ingredients, blending well. Have your favorite chips available for dipping and serve when ready.

CRABS LIKE NEVER BEFORE

Said a nice old madam named Belle
whom the preacher was threatening with Hell,
"I have no regrets—no doubts and no debts
if I haven't done good, I've done well."

Now I know what you're probably thinking, but only if you've had crabs like never before. And we're not talking A-2000 Pyrinate or gasoline and a pack of matches along with an ice pick here.

In a cat house one of the last things you'd think you'd want to have offered to you would be *"crabs like never before."* However, at Fran's Star Ranch (located just north of Beatty, Nevada) this little treat is well received and easy to prepare.

INGREDIENTS

6 English muffins, sliced into halves (makes 12 treats)
1 pound crab meat (or imitation crab meat)
1 pound of Velveeta cheese, grated
1 small can sliced black olives
6 green onions (mostly the tops), chopped
4 tablespoons mayonnaise

You'll want to toast the muffin slices first, then mix all of the above mentioned ingredients together and spread onto the muffin slices. Finally, you'll want to broil the little crab delights until they start to brown on top. Be careful here, and keep a close eye on them, or you'll end up with scorched pizza-ettes instead of *"crabs like never before."*

If you have any questions give Fran a call at her ranch. She's been in the business in Nevada a long time and probably has most of the answers.

CHEESE LOG

When a guy walks into a cat house and the ladies line up to introduce themselves to him, often times what they're looking at is a potential *"cheese log."* Who the hell knows where he's been? The ladies would hope that he's been mostly *"menage a uno,"* but they can never tell. Thank the gods for laws mandating safe sex in brothels. Condoms are mandatory in Nevada bordellos and for all the right reasons. But the guy should not feel intimidated if he's been out in the field a little longer than usual, for these ladies are pros and will clean him up quicker than a four-star chef working lettuce at the Waldorf during lunch.

INGREDIENTS

1/2 cup almonds
1/4 cup pecans
1/4 cut walnuts
1/2 teaspoon cinnamon
1/4 teaspoon ginger
1/8 teaspoon allspice
3/4 cup brown sugar
3 teaspoons water
1 round of Brie cheese

You'll want to chop up the nuts (in a processor if possible) first, then blend with the spices, sugar and water. Next, add a round of Brie cheese (with the rind removed), and broil until it's the consistency of slightly soft goo. When it's all soft, roll it into a log, and *voila,* it's cheese log time.

Chill down and serve when you're ready.

RIKKI'S SPREAD

Rikki likes to play around. She's beautiful, intelligent and available if you're into having a good time. When working she can be found at the Hacienda Ranch in Wells, a place that sports several fine women and an in-house ATM money machine to make paying for the opportunity and experience even easier.

INGREDIENTS

6 ounces goat cheese (shaped into a ball)
6 ounces softened cream cheese
1 tablespoon minced shallot
1/8 cup minced parsley
2 tablespoons minced red pepper
2 cloves minced garlic
1/8 cup minced celery
1/2 teaspoon paprika

Mix the ingredients thoroughly, shaping into a ball, and chill for at least two hours. Serve it with a baguette of French bread or some quality crackers along with a good bottle of red wine.

Rikki has a real tasty spread and encourages you to try it. She also suggests some high fashion fetish when serving this treat. She likes *"tight ass latex neck vest dresses"* (available from the **Mind Candy** catalog people)." A madam whose brothel brought cheers

BROTHEL SPROUTS

Sometimes these ladies work a little too long, and a little too hard, reaching an exhausted state of mind and body, where only lots of sleep and relaxation can help to restore a semblance of well being again for them. They are burned out, crisp fried from working too many late nights and early mornings. Vegetated, of the vegetable family. Hence, the term "brothel sprouts."

But, no matter how cooked they may be, this appeteaser should be prepared *al dente.*

INGREDIENTS

1 pound fresh brussel sprouts
3 tablespoons butter
1/2 fresh lemon

Steam the brussel sprouts until *al dente* (literally "to the tooth"). Chill for one hour, then cut in half lengthwise. Next melt your butter, and saute your sprouts until warm, lastly squeezing in your lemon juice before serving immediately with your finest toothpicks.

A tired young hooker from Nome,
was worn out from toes to her dome.
Ten miners came screwing,
but she said, "Nothing doing —
one of you has got to go home."

TOFU FETISH PATÉ

There once was a hooker from Crete,
who had such a fetish for feet
all she'd eat was toe-fu,
and screw until blue,
screaming "hell with toe-fu, I want meat!"

Jodi from the Stardust likes to have her toes caressed, gently rubbed, squeezed, stroked and sucked upon. She says that if you have any body parts that you would like to have rubbed, squeezed, stroked, or sucked upon too, just pay her a visit and she'll be happy to reciprocate.

In the meantime you'll have to settle for her tofu paté.

INGREDIENTS

1 package of firm tofu
1/2 cup of mayonnaise
2 bunches of cilantro
1 jalapeno pepper
3 pepproncini

Rinse the tofu, then squeeze it between two plates until all the water is drained out. Crumble the tofu into a large mixing bowl. Finely chop all of your other ingredients, then add your mayonnaise until the mixture is at a consistency you prefer.

Refrigerate and chill for two hours before serving on tortilla chips, pita bread or on your favorite body parts.

Breakfast
in Bed

EGGS BEND A DICK

It's first thing in the morning and you're lying in bed. If you're alone you might be conjuring up thoughts of the *"dancing banana,"* a healthy morning fun fruit treat by yourself. However, if someone is beside you, it could be time to explore the possibilities of breakfast in bed with more than just creative sourdough recipes on your mind.

"Rise and shine Mr. Sleepyhead" takes on a whole new meaning here, and what better way to start the day than with this great treat.

INGREDIENTS
6 slices of cooked ham (1/4 inch thick)
3 English muffins, cut in half and toasted
6 poached eggs
Hollandaise sauce (pre-mixed packet from the grocery)
  or you can make it with
3 egg yolks, 1/2 cup melted butter, 2 tablespoons lemon juice
1 tablespoon water and a dash of salt.

Combine and beat the yolks with other ingredients in the top of a double boiler of hot (not boiling!) water using a wire whisk whipper until it starts to get fluffy. Next add softened butter and continue to beat the ingredients into a thick lather (don't let your water boil!). Add 1/2 teaspoon lemon juice and continue to beat until you have a thickened sauce, then set it aside.

In a skillet, brown your ham in some butter, then place the slices on the English muffins, top each with a poached egg and hollandaise sauce. That's it. You're now ready to serve it .

When you walk into the bedroom and say, *"Time to get up,"* chances are he already will be, in anticipation. What better way to make the morning even more special than by dressing for it. Slip into a pair of *"Sweet Cheeks"* panties, body powder down with *"Zodiac Edible Body Powder"* (horoscope included, and available from the **Good Looks Company Catalog**), and casually walk by "Mr. Up," with a breakfast in bed ready to be fully enjoyed.

STACY'S TASTE
OF TEXAS

Stacy is a fine looking cowgirl from just outside Dallas, well versed in Texas charm and hospitality. She says that if you show her your *"Johnson,"* she'll be happy to take you to *"Johnson City and back,"* with a nice taste of Texas in between!

Now what she has in mind here are delicious breakfast cookies that are real sweet with an uncanny ability to help jump-start your morning. And, if you ever get a chance to taste Stacy's cookies I'm sure your battle cry will be more than "Remember the Alamo."

INGREDIENTS

1/3 cup vanilla bean
1/2 cup sifted confectioners sugar
3/4 cup walnuts
1/3 pound butter, left standing at room temperature
1/2 cup granulated sugar
1 1/4 cup flour

Chop the vanilla bean. Pulverize it with your blender adding 1 tablespoon of confectioners sugar, then add the rest of the sugar. Mix with the other ingredients, cover and let stand.

Next, preheat your oven to 350 degrees. Put the walnuts into your food processor and blend them into a paste. Add the butter, sugar and flour, mixing all of the ingredients into a smooth dough. Shape the dough into teaspoon sized crescents (or get a penis shaped cookie cutter to whip them out) and go for it. The cookie cutter is available from the **Erotic Bakery Catalog** referenced in the back of this book.

Bake on an ungreased cookie sheet until light brown (approximately 13-17 minutes), remove and cool from the oven. But while they're still warm, roll them in the prepared vanilla sugar.

Stacy was last seen working at the New Sagebrush Red Light Ranch outside of Carson City, and says that if you want to visit her she'll be happy to share another one of her treats with you!

REAL MEN
EAT KEISHA

Keisha is another fine cooker hooker from the Mustang Ranch. Native American, with Russian blood, spectacular dark eyes and even more beautiful dark hair.

To the French *"quiche"* is a special pie, richly filled with custard and other tasty ingredients. What Keisha has in mind is an equally rewarding taste and enjoyment treat to the senses. But as Keisha says, *"After you've had the custard, cheese, and bacon, you'll be ready to enjoy the best part of the meal."* Real men would love to eat Keisha.

This meal works equally well for breakfast, as an appeteaser, and for lunch, but we include it here because of its inexpensiveness, ease of preparation and timeliness. Early to bed and early to rise!

INGREDIENTS
1 nine inch pre-lined pastry pan (from your grocery store)
3 strips of bacon
1 small onion (or scallion) sliced thin or chopped fine
1/2 cup Swiss cheese, cubed into 1/4 inch balls
1/4 cup Parmesan cheese grated
2 eggs beaten, plus 1 additional egg yolk added and beaten
1/2 cup cream or half & half
1/8 teaspoon nutmeg
Salt & pepper to taste

In a skillet cook your bacon first, then drain off most of the excess grease before you brown your onions. When the onions and bacon are done take them off the oven and break the bacon into small bits, then add the onions and bacon bits along with the eggs, cream, cheese, nutmeg and salt & pepper into the pastry pie dish.

The additional egg yolk at this point adds to the color and richness of the meal, as well as to the cholesterol.

Next, you'll want to bake it approximately 40 minutes, or until the proverbial toothpick inserted into the mixture pulls out clean.

Now, another nice thing about this recipe is that once you put it in the oven you'll have plenty of time to prepare and serve your meal, after which the exploration of another pleasure oven should come into play.

So don't be shy about dressing for the part. A pair of 12" long red serving gloves with white full length stay up stockings, and a soft colored baby doll top should be just about all it takes to put your sex partner over the top.

And, when you're ready to serve this meal the phrase, *"Feel like eating something?"* will take on a whole new meaning and offer up a nice morning experience.

A catalog from **Fredericks of Hollywood** can help attire you in this endeavour. See the references at the back of this book.

There once was a man from St. Paul
who went to a masquerade ball.
He thought he could risk it
to go as a biscuit,
but a hooker ate him up in the hall.

PIGS IN A BLANKET

Sometimes in the morning you're not sure if this recipe is meant to be eaten or referred to in a derogatory manner. Depends on who's doing the talking and who's doing the listening. Quite frankly, *"butt ugly"* can happen to the best of us in the morning and love has nothing to do with it. But don't take it personally, and with a little juice, food, hair brush and toothbrush, the radio could be playing *"Good Morning Starshine"* just as easily as *"What's Love Got To Do With It.."*

"Pigs in a Blanket" is a pretty universal dish. Maybe not always *"pretty,"* but still universal. We're talking oral finger food, wrapped around a pancake and sweetened with a little syrup, jam, or your favorite royal jelly from the queen bee. Butter is optional. And so are whisker biscuits.

One of the better versions of this recipe comes from a good looking lady named Taylor, one of the many beauties that play at the New Sagebrush Ranch. Taylor says that if you provide the sausage she can provide the pleasure.

INGREDIENTS

Bisquick
Eggs
Milk
Butter
Oil
A package of: Sausage links, porkers, big boys, one-eyed jacks, blue throbbers, little hombres, lumber sticks, John Wayne Bobbitt wanna be's, joy sticks, yahoos, closet monsters, one-eyed mambas, magic wands, pleasure weapons, heat seeking missiles, or whatever else you want to call these little meaty morsels.

Taylor recommends Alaskan sourdough pancake starter and reindeer sausage for the ultimate (yet inexpensive) gourmet treat, all of which may be ordered from the Alaska Sausage Company out of Anchorage, Alaska (see reference at back of the book).

The objective is to cook your link sausages first, then place them in the oven on warm while you prepare your pancakes. Real simple stuff here, so make a whole bunch of pancakes and keep those warm too before serving it all up.

When everything is cooked adjourn to the bedroom with a tray full of goodies, along with a container of melted butter and your finest edible toppings.

Orange juice is optional. Perhaps champagne mimosas on your part?

Now, when you wrap the first meaty member around a golden brown pancake, followed by a drip smattering of butter and joy sauce on top, and then gently place it into yours or your partners mouth for starters, this could get exciting. Nothing like a big meaty member wrapped in your hand and gently placed onto your sweet lips to get the morning going.

It's a good idea to have plenty of melted butter, syrup, and whip cream available to add to the tasty festivities. It's also a good idea to realize that this could get messy in bed, hence the term *"pigs in a blanket."*

Believe me, sweet treats are going to be spilled all over the bed on this meal, so tee shirts only are highly recommended. Also, damp wash cloths and towels will play prominent roles in this affair.

But enjoy your breakfast completely. And after it's all over, turn on the TV and watch cartoons. Maybe Porky and Petunia will be on, and you can relive the moment.

This little piggy went to the office,
this little piggy stayed home.
Then each little piggy used whipped cream,
and loved having sex on the foam!

ROBIN'S EGGS
WITH LEGS

This is a little fancier breakfast, involving legs of choice and eggs, almost any way you want them.

Robin, the one with the sensuous Spanish eyes, beautiful body and full inviting lips is credited with this recipe. She spent a lot of time working and playing in the Wells, Nevada area, jumping between the Hacienda Ranch and Donna's as her independence suited her.

When she'd get on the C.B. radio and offer up the following suggestion: "If it swells and you're in Wells stop on by," lots of road-weary travelers would take her up on it. Robin was not an early riser (unlike most of the guys that visited her), but she had a good definition of "chow down," and this meal offers up some nice possibilities.

Here's a tip: Get your supply of goodies ready the night before.

INGREDIENTS

6 eggs
1/2 cup grated mild or sharp Cheddar cheese
Frozen hash browns (unless you want to grate some fresh ones)
1 can of cream of mushroom soup (you know the brand to get!)
1/4 cup brandy
Sliced toast (4-8 pieces)

Cook your hash brown potatoes first and set aside. Then cook your eggs and cheese into an omelette consistency.

Next, heat your soup with the brandy until it begins to boil, then bring to a simmer and cover.

Finally, place the toast on the plates, followed by the eggs and potatoes, next pouring the gravy concoction over it, leaving just enough gravy sauce in the pan to use as *"soppum"* for your extra toast.

Dress wearing an "Arabian Nights" leather halter top draped in chains, along with a leather G-string, available from the **Dream Dresser Catalog,** and deliver your meal on a tray.

Serve with a big wet kiss, have great sex with your partner afterwards, then sleep it off. And, when you wake up, do it again. If it's real good your partner won't even ask about the *"legs"* part of the meal, as that will already have been included and enjoyed.

There once was a lady from Reno
who lost all her money at keno.
But as she lay on her back
and offered a snack,
she knew she'd soon own the Casino.

Soups
& Salads

JAIL HOUSE ROCKS

Prostitution is illegal in a few of Nevada's counties, primarily those with large city populations, including Clark County (Las Vegas), Washoe County (southshore Lake Tahoe), Carson County (the state capital) and Douglas County (Reno), and if people are caught by the police soliciting sex for money they may be arrested, inconvenienced and sentenced to do some jail time at the *"Iron Inn."*

A working girl by the name of Lisa has a better suggestion for doing *"hard time."* It's called making a visit to the Lazy B Guest Ranch, a legal Nevada cat house, where everyone does *"hard time"* and loves it!

And once there, she'll be happy to give you more than a taste of this quick and easy to make salad. Lisa says this is just one of the many things that are fun to eat at the Lazy B.

INGREDIENTS

1 container of Cool Whip (12 ounces)
1 package of orange gelatin
1 pint of cottage cheese
1 package of chopped nuts (16 ounces)
2 small cans of drained mandarin oranges

Blend it all together, chill and serve when ready.

Lisa says that it's great for parties and funerals alike. If you're hungry for more, stop by and say hi!

A pert little hooker named Bobbie,
would stroll through the MGM lobby.
Attracting the stares
of old millionaires,
not entirely, I think, as a hobby.

Black Mask Soup

Marie plays at the Stardust Ranch, a gentleman's social club located in the heart of downtown Ely. It's open from noon until 4 a.m., but if you want to spend the night with Marie (or Tia, Jodi, Tracy or Dallas), it can be arranged. And there's an ATM on-site to help make your withdrawal that much easier.

Ely has a rich mining history along with a flourishing red light district. So if you're into exploring, this just might be the place to start. Marie has long dark curly hair, dark flashing eyes and a great sense of humor. Her recipe is pretty good too.

INGREDIENTS

1/4 cup olive oil
3/4 pound smoked ham
3 Spanish onions, chopped up
1/3 cup minced fresh parsley or cilantro
12 cloves fresh garlic, minced
1 pound black beans, soaked overnight in cold water
8 cups chicken broth stock
3 corn tortillas cut up
2 cups dry red wine
2 bay leaves
2 carrots grated
Tabasco sauce to taste (the hotter the better)
1 tablespoon dried oregano
2 teaspoons cumin powder
Salt and pepper to taste

Heat your oil in a large pan and saute your onions, ham, carrots, parsley and garlic until the onions are brown. Add your beans, chicken stock, wine, tortillas and the other seasonings, bringing to a boil first, then reducing the heat to medium and gradually cooking down for about 30 minutes. Add more liquid if necessary from your bean stock until you're ready to serve it.

Serve when ready in soup bowls, and have additional condiments to add, including bowls of grated cheddar cheese, green chillis, green onions, fresh chopped tomatoes, sour cream, chopped olives, fresh cilantro, and lemon wedges.

Marie likes latex and leather, along with a good time, and recommends attiring yourself accordingly with goodies from the **Demask Catalog,** a company from Holland that puts out wild clothing and masks for your theatrical pleasures and pursuits. See references at the back of the book.

"Of soup and love, the first is best."

—Old Spanish Proverb

"Unless you've been with Marie . . ."

—A visitor to the Stardust Ranch in Ely, Nevada

69 SALAD

The French say *"soisante-neuf,"* the Chinese refer to it as *"two can chew,"* and I'm not sure how other language experts describe the old muncho reversal position. *"Mange"* is another French term, but this meal knows no gender or semantic limitations, and should serve you well for most situations, be it hetero or same sex scenarios.

Whether you're into boy/girl, girl/girl, or mano a mano, the secret to this gender nonspecific almost politically correct *"success"* (and we hoped we spelled it right here) is in the preparation. Be quick, because it only takes sixty-nine seconds to create it, and hence its name.

INGREDIENTS

1 head of red leaf lettuce
Juice from one ripe lemon (squeezed into a bowl with
  seeds removed)
1 large ripe tomato, diced
2 tablespoons olive oil
1 clove garlic, smashed and diced into the wooden salad bowl
1/4 pound bay shrimp (probably pre-frozen) from your local
  meat market counter, pre-shelled, and rinsed several times
  to remove as much of the sea essence smell as possible
2 inches of squeezed anchovy paste lined into bowl
2 baby carrots, grated
Parmesan cheese, freshly grated (approx. 1/4 cup)
Garlic powder, lemon pepper and zesty "Salad Elegance" herb
  powder from your spice rack, if available.

Just work all the ingredients together confidently into a tasty consistency then serve it. What you will discover (regardless of who you're serving it to) is that any concern or worry you or your partner may have had about bad breath will disappear almost immediately (and we're not talking mega doses of retsin drops, breath assures or the binaca blast) because your breaths will now be so intense with garlic, anchovy paste and lemon juice that all forms of self-consciousness will dissipate, and anything after that you might be inclined to taste or indulge in will have the same essence.

Remember, you're both dealing with chomped on garlic, some seasoned bay shrimp, anchovy paste, fresh grated Parmesan cheese and probably a few glasses of alcohol to cut the edge, and *voila*, "69" becomes more than loose leaf lettuce as a possibility.

And, if you enjoy your "69" party afterwards, there's a good chance that some organic dental floss just might be available too.

Ashes to ashes,
Dust to dust,
Oil that dick
Before it rusts.

WHIPS AND CHAINS SALAD

This recipe came from one nice looker, part time hooker extraordinaire. Her name is Brandi, and she has a sense of humor to match her beauty. Last seen working and playing at the New Sagebrush Red Light Ranch.

INGREDIENTS

1 man
1 woman
1 set of handcuffs from your local handcuff purveyor
1 blindfold
1 leather mask
2 riding crops
1 T-9 ball gag trainer (it looks like a red hand ball strapped in your mouth, worn by Bruce Willis in the film "Pulp Fiction," during an uncomfortable moment)
2 sensual nipple pinchers
1 cock ring

Well now, you've got the ingredients for this little low calorie feast. Put them all together in a ratio balance that makes you feel comfortable, but Brandi suggests that you show some imagination when attiring yourself for these occasions. Wigs, makeup, jewelry, leather, etc., can enhance the atmosphere tremendously. Put some XXX in your excitement at meal time!

There was a young lady who knew
she had chosen the wrong thing to do.
But she did it so well, she owned a hotel
in Las Vegas before she was through.

FORBIDDEN FRUIT SALAD

There was a young hooker from Kent,
who claimed not to know what they meant.
When men asked her age,
she'd reply in a rage,
"My age is the age of consent."

The mind can play strange tricks, often times leading many of us astray. Forbidden fruit, what can you be thinking? Pederasty, a cousin, niece or nephew? Possibly someone of questionable age (yours and theirs)? If you have to ask, play it safe and *don't ask!*

Head instead into the kitchen and prepare this little taste treat. It's healthy for mind, body and spirit, after which you'll feel so good about yourself that you'll want to celebrate in some bacchanalian manner. Wine and revelry should parallel this course. The only fruits that will be forbidden are those that are out of season.

INGREDIENTS

1 package of grated coconut
Fresh strawberries
Fresh pineapple
Mango
Papaya
Kiwi
Bananas
Melon
Berries
Peaches
Grapes
Oranges

Ambrosia is the food of the gods and immortals, and in the right quantities the fruits mentioned above will treat you just as royally. Hand pick your fruit from your favorite vendor or grocer. Whichever ingredients and quantities you decide to use is pretty much up to you. Just make sure everything is peeled, cut or diced into edible size bites.

When you have prepared the above mentioned ingredients dump them all into a large bowl and chill in the refrigerator until you're ready to serve.

At serving time you'll want to top off your Forbidden Fruit Salad with a one pint container of whipped cream (or nonfat substitute), and then add 1/2 cup of peach brandy liqueur. Blend well, serve, and enjoy the moments to follow.

DENISE'S NOODLE DOODLE

Denise has a good recipe here. In fact, she has a good recipe for life. She says to write a blue print for the relationship you want, because you will get it. This first-class working woman conducts her pleasure at the New Sagebrush Red Light Ranch, five miles east of Carson City, in the *"Golden Triangle,"* and has plenty of insight and heritage to back her up: Spanish, German and Italian, with the ability to put you into a comfort level visualizing topless sandy beaches and tradewinds blowing three shades of blue past your mind. Noodle doodle indeed!

But, she cautions, if you're not in shape, and allow too much alcohol and hot tub activity to overcome you, the story line could become noodle dangle instead of soak and poke, so take care here and keep it up.

INGREDIENTS

1 pound wide noodles
3 tablespoons olive oil
1/4 cup chopped parsley
1/4 cup diced almonds (for texture)
1/4 pound sliced mushrooms
1/4 cup grated Parmesan cheese
1 tablespoon lemon juice

Basic floor plan here, according to Denise. Cook your noodles and drain, then gradually add the other ingredients, blending well. When done preparing this complex carbohydrate delight refrigerate until ready.

AFTERNOON THAI DELIGHT

This is not exactly your typical *"nooner"* with your next door neighbor. It's something much more special than that. This will be impressive...something you will want to dress for. This opportunity needs to be planned out.

Exotic attire: Where *"Thai"* takes on a whole new meaning, involving some hardware along with the silverware, and perhaps some *"discipline"* on your part.

Whipped cream, insatiable appetites, lots of leather, latex...you'll want to be on top of the situation and well prepared. A binding relationship could be involved. Passion comes alive with this treat: Thai cucumber salad.

INGREDIENTS
4 nice looking cucumbers
5 tablespoons white wine vinegar
6 tablespoons sugar
3/4 cup water
Salt and fresh ground pepper to taste
2 tablespoons of finely diced seeded hot green peppers

Rinse and gently peel your cucumbers, then cut them in half lengthwise and scrape out the seeds. Cut the slices into finer pieces and add your diced hot peppers.

Next, blend the white wine vinegar, sugar, water, salt and pepper over a mild heat. Keep stirring until the sugar is completely dissolved, then pour it over the cucumbers. Leave at room temperature until cool, then refrigerate. Serve with finely ground coriander seeds on top (1/3 teaspoon).

A TASTE FROM DOWN UNDER

Tammie is another expert in her craft, and knows a lot about getting down and going down under. With inventiveness and skill rivaled only by her charm and beauty, this babe is from New Zealand, where *"down under"* has a whole different meaning. We're talking primordial and subterranean. Dark, enigmatic and musky odors. Sweet essence of dampness and desire.

What Tammie has in mind here is mystical and obscure, involving the pursuit of the morchella (morel) mushroom in esoteric forests. Delicate, earthy pleasures from down under, brought to fruition in a delectable mushroom soup. Tammie knows that there is only one other edible item that tastes as good as a morel mushroom which also comes from down under. She recommends getting down and checking it out. Or, stop by and visit her at Mabel's Whorehouse outside Las Vegas.

INGREDIENTS

2 cups (approximately 1 pound) of morel mushrooms (fresh, frozen, or dried . . . see reference at back of book to get them)
1 quart cold water
4 tablespoons of butter
2 sweet onions, chopped into little bits
1/3 cup dry red wine
1 cup chicken broth stock
2 cups water
1/2 teaspoon celery salt
Salt and pepper to taste
1 cup cream
3 egg yolks
1 bag of croutons, and several lemon wedges for garnish

You want to soak your morels overnight in water, remembering to retain the water stock afterwards. This stuff is good, and you want to be able to incorporate it later into your final product.

After your morels have been soaked overnight, pat them dry and saute them in the butter for about five minutes.

Next pour in your red wine (pouring a glass for yourself too), add the celery salt, followed by the chicken stock and morel water stock before simmering over low heat for about 10 minutes. Add your salt and pepper to taste.

In a separate bowl blend your cream and egg yolks together, and when it's well blended, begin to add it gradually to the morel soup stock. Continue to heat, but don't let it boil.

Serve when ready, along with lemon wedges and paprika as garnish.

After this meal from Down Under,
go nuts, have great sex, and plunder...
Mushrooms of magic —
it would be tragic,
to run out of this sexual wonder!

There once was a horny mechanic,
who often became quite manic.
He'd dip his wick,
instead of the stick,
and "checking your oil" became frantic.

There once was a lady named Mabel,
so ready, so willing, so able.
And so full of spice,
she could name her own price.
Now Mabel's all wrapped up in sable.

TUESDAY'S CAT HOUSE SPECIAL

Tuesday is a dark skinned talent that works at Mabel's Whore House in Crystal, Nevada. Blue eyes, and long, long legs that don't quit. She doesn't quite have her own zip code yet, but Tuesday can definitely take you into Wednesday without any jet lag. She says this recipe has the ability to lift your spirits along with other body parts. It's a cold avocado soup that should make your dinner guests green with envy.

INGREDIENTS

2 large ripe avocados
1/2 cup plain yogurt or cream
1- 1/2 cups chicken broth
Salt and pepper to taste
A splash of good white wine (Chardonnay or Riesling)
  or sherry
Lemon slices for garnish

Slice your avocados in half, retaining 1/2 avocado on the side while mashing the others in a bowl with your yogurt to a fine pureed consistency.

Next heat your chicken stock to boiling, then gradually stir in the avocado puree, while also adding your salt and pepper and the splash of white wine (remembering to pour a glass for yourself at the same time).

When all is blended well remove from the heat and serve either hot or cold, with avocado slices and lemon wedges as garnish on top.

Dinners

PASTA PUTTANESCA BROTHELCELLI

The miners came in '49
The whores in '51
And when they got together,
they produced the native son.

... They also produced an efficient and easy to prepare meal for their late night customers called "Pasta Puttanesca Brothelcelli" (with freshly choked and fried chicken).

INGREDIENTS

3 tablespoons of olive oil
2 cans crushed tomatoes
4 garlic cloves minced
6 black olives sliced
6 green olives sliced
3 tablespoons capers, wet and sticky
4 anchovy fillets... hand patted dry and chopped
1/4 bunch parsley chopped
2 tablespoons fresh basil chopped
4 boneless, skinless, naked hen breasts, cubed and fried
1 pound spaghetti

Heat the olive oil in a pan and brown your garlic first. Then add olives, tomatoes, capers and anchovy fillets, stirring well and cooking for 5-8 minutes. In a separate pan fry your chicken pieces.

Cook the pasta and drain it. Next place your pasta in a bowl and add half the sauce, blending well. Finally add the remaining sauce on top and sprinkle on the parsley. Serve when ready.

LISA'S LOVER'S LASAGNA

Lisa is 5'10" of lovable woman with blonde hair and deep green eyes that express a mischievous and playful attitude about life. To fully appreciate her, a trip to the Lazy B Guest Ranch is in order for a taste of some unique *fantasy cuisine.*

The Lazy B is located just outside the town of Fallon, across the road from the Naval Flight Squadron training base. Carrier Air Groups come here to practice their techniques, and many aviators have perfected several moves here above and beyond the call of duty including *"Arm Your Weapon," "Cat Launch," "Pulling 13 G's," and "Splash Two Bogies."* These are "Top Gun" ace pilot moves and Lisa is well versed in most of them. She wants her air jockeys to be careful, but one thing she never cautions them to do is *"Pull out!"*

INGREDIENTS

16 ounces lasagna noodles
3 cups crab meat (from crab legs or imitation)
1 pound chopped broccoli pieces
2 cups grated carrots
1 cup chopped onions
3 cups canned (drained) tomatoes
1 pound thinly sliced fresh mushrooms
1 teaspoon dried oregano
1 tablespoon dried parsley
1 tablespoon finely chopped fresh garlic
2 cups Parmesan cheese, finely grated
Salt and ground pepper to taste
A splash or two or three of red wine

In a frying pan add 3-5 tablespoons of olive oil and begin to brown your carrots, onions and mushrooms. Next add your tomatoes along with the oregano, parsley, garlic and red wine. Cook down into a fine consistency.

In a separate pan boil your broccoli pieces until tender, then cook your noodles.

In a 12" x 12" x 3" baking pan you're going to want to layer your noodles first, then your broccoli bits, then tomato sauce, then cover with Parmesan cheese, then another noodle layer, followed by the crab meat, then tomato sauce, then Parmesan cheese, then noodles again, followed by the rest of the sauce and Parmesan cheese.

Bake 15-20 minutes at 350 F., and serve hot with French bread, red wine, and follow it with a hot lavender massage.

ALFREDO FETE A WEENIE

O.K., this sharp recipe came from an even sharper lady working down at the Cherry Patch Ranch just outside Las Vegas. Her name is Sindee. She enjoys fantasies, and extends an open invitation to those guys out there who want their weenies feted. She said you might be her next Prince Charming or *"Sir Lance A Lot"* invited to the ultimate grand ball. Tall, leggy, dark haired, with deep blue eyes, full passionate lips, and a warm inviting smile, Sindee offers the following recipe:

INGREDIENTS

1 pound fettucine pasta
1/4 pound butter
1 cup half & half
1/3 pound grated Parmesan cheese
Salt & pepper to taste

Cook your noodles in a big pot of boiling water for 4-5 minutes. Drain and place to one side.

Next, in a pan you want to put the noodles and add your other ingredients, heating and mixing as you go. Add your salt and pepper to taste. When the cheese has melted completely you're ready to serve.

Now, because this is a relatively easy dish to prepare without too much fuss, dress for it. Sindee suggests a sheer power net Teddy, T-back style rear with zipper front. **Dream Dresser Catalog** has just the item. See references at the back of the book.

SUNNY'S NOODLE DELIGHT

Sunny is a blonde haired, blue eyed party animal working out at the Cherry Patch II, which is the closest brothel to Las Vegas on Highway 95. She is one of the most diverse and multi-talented women to have ever played in a cat house, with Sapphic charms and insights. If you're in the mood for a little noodle delight, Sunny just might have the right recipe for you, be it same sex or hetero!

INGREDIENTS

1 pound lean ground beef
1 clove minced garlic
2 tomatoes diced up
1 yellow onion chopped up
Olive oil
1 cup of grated (food processed if possible) Parmesan cheese

Saute your garlic and onions in the olive oil first, then toss in your tomatoes. In a separate pan brown your ground beef, gradually adding some of the tomato sauce to it. Boil your noodles separately.

Put the meat in a casserole plate blending the noodles in with it. Take your Parmesan cheese at this point and sprinkle on top, then place the meal in the oven for 10 minutes at 350 degrees.

Finally you'll want to brown the crust at broiler temperature until it's firm and dark, but not burned. Serve when ready.

There was a young harlot named Sunny,
whose kisses were sweeter than honey.
Her callers galore, lined up at the door,
to take turns in paying her money.

Hard Core Tacos & Testosterone Tostados

"Here's to the fire that doesn't bring down shacks and and shanties... but brings down pants and panties!"

—Tyler, hooker cooker at The New Sagebrush Red Light Ranch

Tyler is another one of the many beautiful women that work at the New Sagebrush, about five miles east of the Nevada capital building in Carson City. She likes her food like she enjoys her sexual experiences: hot and spicy, and these two recipes will help confirm that.

Her hot sauce will work for all the basics. It you get a chance to visit her at the New Sagebrush Red Light Ranch, it could get even hotter.

INGREDIENTS FOR HOT SAUCE

1/2 cup finely chopped jalapeno peppers with seeds
1/2 cup finely chopped onions
3 cups diced tomatoes (fresh or canned)
1/4 cup wine vinegar
2 garlic cloves minced
2 tablespoons lime juice
2 medium sized ripe avocados, diced fine
1 tablespoon olive oil
2 tablespoons finely chopped parsley
2 teaspoons chopped basil
1 teaspoon thyme
1 teaspoon oregano

Combine all of the ingredients well, as this will be your base for the tacos and tostados. And best of all, you can put it in or on virtually anything you want, from leftovers to fresh foods. *Continued*

With tacos you can use either corn or flour tortillas, however with tostados, flour tortillas are recommended by Tyler.

Fresh grated head lettuce
Shredded beef, chicken, or cheddar cheese
Refried beans

Heat and bend your tortillas in a hot pan with a little cooking oil in it, shape them when ready, and fill with the goods, adding your hot sauce on top for the ultimate eye and nostril opener.

For tostados you can be even more creative by cleaning out your refrigerator and sinus passages:

Fresh grated head lettuce
Shredded beef, chicken or cheddar cheese
Refried beans
Canned corn nibblets
Diced black olives
Chopped up tomatoes

Tostados are heated briefly, but served flat, with the above mentioned ingredients added on top before the hot sauce is mixed in with it. Think of it as a big salad on a flat tortilla.

These two recipes can create a mess in your kitchen with lots of slicing, chopping and dicing preparation, but they're erotic, and can help conjure up images of other hot and spicy mouth-watering treats to follow. For enchiladas this killer hot sauce will work wonders here too, and this idea comes from a good looking lady named Brandi, a talent who's been known to call The New Sagebrush her home now and again. She encourages inquiring minds to stop on by for additional insights.

Brandi says to shred cooked chicken and cheese on your tortillas (uncooked). Then roll the cheesy globs of goo lengthwise before placing them onto a baking dish (with some hot sauce coating the bottom of the dish), and pouring the remaining hot sauce over the enchiladas. Bake at 325 degrees for 20-25 minutes and serve hot.

THE TWILIGHT BONE

Submitted for your approval by Jamie at Donna's Ranch in Wells: It could be early evening when you unlock this door with the key of imagination. Beyond it is another dimension...a dimension of sound, a dimension of sight...a dimension of mind, body and matter. You're moving into a land of both shadow and substance, of food and sexuality. Go as far as you like on this road, as its limits are only those you impose. Your next stop: *"The Twilight Bone."*

INGREDIENTS

A fair sized pork roast (about 4 pounds)
Salt and pepper to taste
1 cup chicken stock
1 bottle of a tasty red wine (Merlot or Cabernet)

Preheat your oven to 450 degrees, open the bottle of wine, pour a glass for you and your lover and wait for the oven to heat up. Gently rub the pork with salt and pepper and place it in a roasting pan ready for the oven.

When the oven's ready put the meat in and cook for about 30 minutes, then reduce the heat to 300 degrees.

Depending on how you want the meat done, use this time guide provided by Jamie: For rare meat, cook the pork approximately 20 minutes per pound; for medium-rare pork, cook approximately 22 minutes per pound; and for well done pork, 27 minutes per pound.

With this in mind you'll be cooking for at least two hours, and drinking about as long, which should give you plenty of time to work up a pretty good heater, and even do a little partying before the meal with your sex partner.

Jamie suggests wearing a flowing glamour robe lavished with soft lace ruffles and a cascading hemline, with flared sleeves and delicate lace edging throughout and, with nothing on underneath. She says this will help to excite your lover's desire for pork. Available from **Fredericks of Hollywood** catalog.

BRITNIE'S RUMP ROAST

"A brothel is a lot like a restaurant because you're always cooking, only not in the kitchen."

—Britnie, classy working gal from P.J.'s Lucky Strike.

Britnie is an attractive blonde with blue eyes that works from time to time at P.J.'s Lucky Strike in Elko, Nevada. She's been to culinary art school in Seattle, and knows more than just a few things about cooking basics, sauces, table decor, and how to use your knife properly.

"A good tip to remember," said Britnie, "so you don't lose one, is to make sure you know where your fingers are at all times." And speaking of losing one, while in a "line up" she cajoled one indecisive gent by saying, "I'm Mrs. Bobbitt, use it or lose it!"

INGREDIENTS

A 4-5 pound rump roast
2 cups chopped onions
Salt to taste
6 strips bacon
1/3 cup wine vinegar
1 tablespoon flour

Preheat your oven to 325, then cook your bacon in a large roasting pan, after which you'll toss in and saute your onions. Next you'll want to add your rump roast, wine vinegar and enough water to cover the bottom of the pan by at least 1 inch.

Bake until your meat is tender, approximately two hours, basting as needed.

When it's done remove from the pan, and make a gravy with your flour and a little more water, cooking the juices until they thicken into a nice consistency.

KYRA'S TONGUE

*"With skill, she vibrates
her eternal tongue."*

— Edward Young

Law student by day, classy hooker by night, with looks like Mariah Carey. Clear eyes and flawless complexion. Can we talk? Kyra likes to get oral, and says the tongue is an organ that can play sweet music. Music is universal...so is sex, meditation and contemplation.

INGREDIENTS

1 large beef tongue (4-5 pounds)
2 onions
1 complete celery stalk
1 bunch parsley
6 carrots
1 bay leaf
1 tablespoon salt
Ground pepper to taste

Make sure your tongue is washed and cleaned, then place it in a huge pot along with your other ingredients and cover with water. Bring to a rolling boil (removing any scum that forms on top) then lower the temperature to simmer for 3 1/2 hours (about 45 minutes per pound).

When the tongue is cooked and tender let it cool down, then take a sharp paring knife to it, removing the thick skin. You may then serve it either hot or cold with the vegetables along with horseradish, mustard and potatoes.

Beef Jerky
Stir Fry

Donna came up with this recipe. She *"cooks"* at Inez's D & D (which stands for *"diddle & daddle"*) in Elko, Nevada. This cat house has been recently rebuilt from the ground up, and is always worth a visit when passing through town. Donna doesn't need to be rebuilt, and is also worth visiting when passing through Elko. She says that beef jerky stir fry is one of her specialties.

Donna cautioned me that this is not your typical beef jerky kind of encounter. It's best when you take your clothes off and eat it. It can be a finger licking good experience to make any meal complete.

INGREDIENTS
1 pound flank steak
1 tablespoon cornstarch
1 egg white
1 tablespoon olive oil
1/4 cup vegetable oil
1/4 cup red wine
6 green onions chopped up
Ground pepper to taste

Slice your raw meat into thin strips first, then place in a bowl along with the cornstarch, egg white and olive oil, massaging in all the ingredients.

Heat the oil in a wok and add the beef, cooking quickly, then removing, while leaving as much oil in the wok as possible. Next add your chopped onions and two tablespoons of red wine, cooking for thirty seconds.

Finally, put the beef back into the wok along with the remaining wine and pepper. Cook for another 30 seconds and you're ready to serve.

MONA LISA'S MEAT LOAF

More than a beautiful painting with a quizzical smile, she is the embodiment and personification of female art, last seen smiling at the Shady Lady, Nevada's newest brothel, located midway between Beatty and Tonepah on Highway 95. She is an excellent cook, and has some great advice about meat loaf: *"Don't let yours!"*

INGREDIENTS

1 pound lean ground beef
1/2 pound ground veal
1/2 pound ground pork
2 eggs
1/4 cup coarsely chopped green pepper
1/2 cup bread crumbs
1/2 cup chopped fresh parsley
1/2 cup chopped fresh chives
1 tablespoon dried basil
Salt and pepper to taste
6 slices of bacon
1 can of tomato sauce

Pre heat your oven to 350 degrees and while it's getting hot mix all your other ingredient together in a bowl with the exception of your bacon slices which you will use to cover your meat loaf ball.

Put it in a baking pan and cook for ninety minutes until done. Serve with your tomato sauce over it.

*"Don't ever let your
meat loaf."*

—Recommendation from Mona Lisa at Shady Lady

BEARDED CLAMS
WITH LINGUINI

Dallas from the Stardust Gentlemen's Club in Ely, Nevada came up with this treat.

INGREDIENTS

1 medium sized onion
1 clove garlic
1 package linguini pasta noodles
1 small can of chopped clams
1 cup dry white wine
3 Roma tomatoes
Olive oil
Basil, oregano and rosemary to taste
Salt and pepper to taste
Parsley
1 dozen fresh baby clams (to be steamed)

This takes common sense proportions and basics. Saute your onion and chopped garlic until brown in your frying pan, while boiling your noodles in a double steamer with the fresh clams in the bottom and the linguini in the top.

Add the can of clams (and its juice) to the onion and garlic on high heat, and then toss in your 1 cup of white wine while pouring another cup for yourself. Cook for about 20 minutes, gradually reducing the juice in your pan. Add your basil, oregano, rosemary, salt and pepper to taste.

When your steamed clams start to open up take them and the linguini off the stove. Finally, add your diced Roma tomatoes to the white wine sauce and cook gently for 3-4 more minutes.

Serve by placing your noodles on plates, pour your linguini sauce over the noodles, and place your fresh steamed clams around the outer sides of the serving plates.

Flat Back Special

Stormy at the Old Bridge Ranch eight miles east of Reno is a specialist at this one. She says that if you like this for dinner you should also try her dessert called *"Stormy Night Delight"*

INGREDIENTS

3 pounds baby back pork ribs
Garlic seasoning
Lemon pepper
Salt to taste

You want to par boil or trim the excess fat off your uncooked ribs (which should be about 1 pound or so per person you plan on feeding), then salt and pepper them before placing them in an oven at 350 degrees for one hour.

Remove from heat and serve when ready with corn on the cob.

Hanna Bantry
in the pantry
gnawing a pork chop bone.
How she gnawed it,
how she clawed it,
when she found herself alone.

CAT HOUSE CATFISH

April is a well equipped gal from the South who enjoys cooking, fishing, and sex, although not necessarily in that order. She says fish is her specialty, and when not working at the Cherry Patch Ranch near Las Vegas she can be found in her New Orleans' kitchen or out in the bayou country with her fishing pole in hand. She could probably do wonders with your pole, too. April has a pretty open mind about most things, and says the only bad fish she doesn't want to see in a cat house is a form of trouser trout known as *"Moby Dick."*

INGREDIENTS

Oil for frying
3/4 cup of cornmeal
Salt and pepper to taste
2 pounds of catfish fillets

Heat the oil for frying and while it's getting to the sizzle point mix your cornmeal, salt and pepper to coat your fillets in.

Cook the fillets in the sizzling oil for 7-10 minutes, depending on their thickness, until they are crisp and brown. Remove and serve with lemon wedges.

*"Moby Dick is the only fish
that's not welcome in a brothel."*

—April, working woman and philosopher

BAMBI'S
PINK SNAPPER

Bambi works and plays at Mabel's Whorehouse, just north of Las Vegas. She loves to go fishing, be it deep blue waters off the coast of California or Baja, or simple trout fishing on some clear water stream in Idaho or Montana. If you see her, just ask, because she probably has a great fishing spot in mind for you, too. Her motto for trout fishing is *"Love them and leave them,"* but you just might be a keeper!

INGREDIENTS

3 pounds of pink snapper fillets
1/3 cup vegetable oil
4 tablespoons butter
3 tablespoons lemon juice
Lemon wedges
3 tablespoons chopped parsley
Flour
Salt and pepper to taste

Bambi says to roll the snapper fillets in the flour, salt and pepper, to coat both sides evenly.

Next, heat the oil in a pan and cook the fish until browned on both sides, approximately 4-5 minutes. You can tell when it's done when the fish meat starts to pull away while testing it with a fork.

In a separate pan melt your butter and add the lemon juice while mixing gently. When all is ready, pour the melted butter and lemon juice over your fish fillets. Serve it up with the lemon wedges and parsley as garnish.

Bambi suggests that when thinking fish food, think fish attire: Sheer black fishnet body stocking with lace halter collar and low scoop back (from the ***Playboy Catalog***), spiked heels, fish hook earrings, a men's white button down shirt with hand painted fish themed silk tie, along with a pierced body part or two.

Tatoos, too, are nice. But if you don't have a couple of real nasty ones, there are catalog listings in the back of this book for ordering a wide selection of temporary stick-ons.

This probably isn't going to be your ordinary "catch and release" party here, but if you do it right, the person you're hooking will be coming up stream faster than you can say, *"Feel like tasting some mighty fine snapper?"* Enjoy!

All men ultimately
bring pleasure in a cat house:
many by coming,
many by leaving.

MICHELLE'S GUMBO

RIDDLE: "What does John Derek do at night
after he takes out his teeth?"

ANSWER: "Gum Bo."

(It's a joke!)

Michelle at the New Sagebrush Red Light Ranch is credited with
this recipe.

INGREDIENTS

2 packages of chicken wings
3 whole crabs
2 pounds dry shrimp
"Gumbo Filet" seasoning sauce
2 cans of large stewed tomatoes
A big pot of cooked white rice

De-bone your chicken wings and boil (about 15-20 minutes) until
tender. Toss in your crabs and shrimp, and cook those next. Finally heat up
your tomatoes, and blend it all together with your white rice.

Serve when ready.

TASTES LIKE CHICKEN

The French translation for *"Coq au vin"* is "Cock with wine," which is how Kayla at the Cherry Patch Ranch refers to it these days. She says she thoroughly enjoys it, too! Kayla says that if you like this idea, she has got another one for "Chicken Crotchitori" that might also blow you away.

INGREDIENTS

1 frying chicken (3 pounds)
1/2 pound small onions
1/2 pound mushrooms
1/2 cup scallions, chopped up
1 clove of garlic, minced
6 slices of bacon
2 tablespoons flour
3 tablespoons of butter
2 cups dry red wine
3 parsley sprigs
1 bay leaf
4 tablespoons of chopped parsley
5 dashes of thyme

Quarter your chicken then salt and pepper to taste. Cook your bacon retaining the fat in the pan, then saute the chicken until brown on all sides.

Next add your onions and mushrooms, cooking slowly until brown and tender. Remove the chicken and add your scallions and garlic, cooking for one minute or so. Blend in your flour, add your wine (while pouring yourself a glass, too), and return the heat to boiling.

Put the chicken back in the pan and add your remaining ingredients. Cover the pan, reduce the heat to simmer and cook for another 30 minutes or until tender.

Remove from the stove, pour the juices over the chicken parts, and serve when ready.

EBONY THIGHS

Toy is her name, and fun is her game. And speaking of beautiful ebony thighs, she's got them. Toy likes to play at Mabel's Whorehouse outside of Las Vegas, and says that if you're in the area and want a free limousine ride to her place of business, just give a call and she'll take care of the rest.

INGREDIENTS
6 chicken thighs
Garlic powder to taste
Lemon pepper to taste
Salt to taste

Preheat your oven to 400 degrees, remove the skins from your chicken thighs before washing them, then powder them with your garlic powder, lemon pepper and salt.

Place on a baking pan and cook for approximately 55 minutes. Serve when ready along with a fresh tossed green salad, potatoes and garlic bread.

A gourmet challenged me to eat
a tiny bit of rattlesnake meat,
remarking, "Don't look so horror-stricken,
you'll find it tastes a lot like chicken."
It did. Now chicken I cannot eat,
because it tastes like rattlesnake meat!

— Ogden Nash

WAM BAM THANK YOU MAM TURKEY

Celeste is a sex worker at Inez's in Elko. She is mostly Hawaiian and Polynesian, renowned for her good looks, charm, personality, etc., etc. Celeste can also give you the best lei you've ever had.

INGREDIENTS

1 pound lean ground turkey
1 pound broccoli
1 12 ounce can of tomato sauce
1 12 ounce can of corn nibblets
1 garden green pepper sliced
3 medium sized potatoes boiled and mashed
Herbal seasonings to taste
Salt and pepper to taste
1 cup of grated medium to sharp cheddar cheese

In a baking dish blend all of the above ingredients except for the grated cheese, and cook for 1 hour at 325 degrees.

After this goodie has cooked for one hour remove it from the oven, sprinkle on top your grated cheddar cheese, and put back into the oven until it melts and starts to turn golden brown.

Remove and serve, singing "Lei Lady Lei."

PORK IN BUNS

Bunny's a luscious lady with perky eyes and a porky bustiere. She offers this simple, but hearty fare. This is also known as *"hide the weenie"* or the *"tube steak special,"* and it's about as basic as it gets.

INGREDIENTS

1 package of all-beef hot dogs
1 package of hot dog buns

Boil the tubes until completely cooked. Serve with buns amidst your favorite condiments.

Here is where Bunny really relishes spreading your ketchup, mustard and pickles on firm, white buns. She suggests donning a French maid's apron with crotchless panties and six inch spiked heels to get those hot dog juices flowing.

•

There once was a girl named Bunny
who thought that her name wasn't funny.
Till she grew up to be,
a rabbit, you see,
and now the boys give her their money.

—Bunny, working girl

WOK ON THE WILD SIDE

Suzie Wong can do no wrong when it comes to this recipe. Young, beautiful and well mannered, if you meet her and she greets you with *"Have you eaten yet?,"* I'm sure you'll want to try more than her fortune cookies. For a different kind of *"wok on the wild side"* visit Suzie at Mabel's Whorehouse in Crystal, Nevada.

INGREDIENTS

1 pound snow peas
2 whole chicken breasts, boned but with skin left on
2 tablespoons cornstarch
4 tablespoons sherry wine
10 small shitaki mushrooms
2 tablespoons soy sauce
2 teaspoons sugar
1 cup vegetable oil
2 teaspoons water

Cut your chicken up into small bite size chunks and place them in a bowl with 1 tablespoon of cornstarch and 1 tablespoon of sherry wine, coating the chicken chunks as you go.

Next soak your mushrooms in hot water for about 30 minutes, then drain and remove any excess liquid.

Combine the soy sauce with sugar and remaining sherry and stir in the last of the cornstarch. This will be your soy sauce mixture that you'll add to the wok in a little bit.

Heat your oil in the wok and cook your chicken bits over a high heat here (about 3-5 minutes). Remove chicken and saute your mushrooms and snow peas for about 1 minute, then toss the chicken back in along with the soy sauce mixture, cooking and stirring for about 30 more seconds. Remove and serve, humming *"Wok on By."*

SPANK
YOUR TUNA

Keri says that if you value your ability to sit down, you do not want to annoy her. She is equally adept with hand, hairbrush, shoe tree and riding crop, and suggests a little discipline training might be in store for you if you visit her at Mabel's Whorehouse. If not, she suggests that you at least try her version of *"Black and Bleu Tuna."*

INGREDIENTS

2 yellow tuna fillets (about 9 ounces each)
1/4 cup Cajun Magic Spice
4 tablespoons butter
1 tablespoon wasabi powder (available at Oriental
   or fine grocery stores)
2 tablespoons soy sauce
Non-stick vegetable oil spray

The objective is simple: you are going to sear and blacken the exterior of the fish, while leaving the interior of the fish pink (the French call it *"bleu"*).

Preheat a cast iron pan on high heat. Next coat both sides of the tuna fillets with the Cajun Magic Spice and prepare to sear them in a pan. But the trick is not to burn the fish, so spray each piece with the nonstick vegetable spray before dropping them into the hot pan.

Prepare your butter, wasabi paste, and soy sauce in little dipping bowls, and have them ready when your fish is done.

Sear the fish for 1 minute on each side, remove from the pan, slice into thin strips, and serve immediately.

Tip: If you have to whip up your own "Cajun spice", make it *"ragin"*.

(See next page for Cajun Spice Mixture)

CAJUN SPICE MIXTURE

2 tablespoons paprika
1 tablespoon salt
1 tablespoon onion powder
1 tablespoon garlic powder
1 tablespoon cayenne pepper
2 teaspoons thyme
1 tablespoon oregano
Ground black pepper to taste

Combine and mix all the ingredients together. Look out, because this stuff is hot, hot, hot. So is Keri.

BUTT
DELIGHT

Beautiful cheeks and calipygian charms most aptly describe Monica as one of the foxy ladies that plies her trade at the Old Bridge Ranch a few minutes drive east of Reno in the community of Mustang, Nevada. Jet black hair, soft white complexion, blue eyes and full red lips, this Kentucky free spirit knows a thing or two about life, with an insight into astrology and the occult. If you're into the stars and heavens, stop by and visit her, because she's got a pretty good answer for the *"Big Bang Theory."* And, in the meantime, try her recipe for some tasty butt.

INGREDIENTS

2 halibut steaks (1 inch thick)
1 minced shallot
1/3 cup mushrooms
A bottle of good California dry white wine
Juice from 1/2 lemon
1 tablespoon chopped parsley
Salt and pepper to taste

Preheat the oven to 400 degrees, and pour yourself a glass of white wine for starters.

Next, saute your shallots and mushrooms in a pan with two table-spoons of butter until they start to brown, then add a couple splashes of wine and the chopped parsley, cooking it down until most of the liquid has evaporated.

Place your two butt steaks on a coated baking dish, and spoon your pan drippings over them. Bake 14-17 minutes until it's cooked to a flaky consistency which easily pulls apart when you put a fork to the butt.

Serve when ready.

Desserts

KYRA'S
TEMPTATION

Kyra has a lot to tempt you with. It could be a look, her smile, or a simple greeting, like: "Want a little dessert?" Let me say just this, if she were on the menu at the Donner Party's last supper banquet she would be the first selection taken. Her orange mocha cake would be a close second.

INGREDIENTS

1 package of Devil's Food Cake Mix (18 ounces approximate)
1 package (4 ounces) chocolate flavor pudding and pie filling mix
4 eggs
3/8 cup vegetable oil
3/4 cup sour cream
1-1/2 cups semisweet chocolate chips
3/8 cup water
1/4 cup coffee flavored liqueur
3 tablespoons finely grated orange rind peelings
Powdered sugar to taste

You're going to preheat your oven to 350 degrees and begin to blend in a bowl the devil's food cake mix, pudding mix, eggs, oil, sour cream, water, liqueur and grated orange peelings for a few minutes, then gradually add your chocolate chips, blending it all nicely together.

Next pour it into a greased and floured cake pan, baking until it is done (about 50 minutes or so, when you can insert a toothpick into it and pull it out cleanly). Let it cool down. Then sift your powdered sugar over it.

THE KAT'S MEOW

Kat is another party animal currently playing at the Mustang Ranch outside of Reno, Nevada. Built like a "10," tall and gorgeous, with eyes that glow blue to green depending upon her mood. She looks like a Dallas Cowboy cheerleader, only she does her rooting elsewhere.

INGREDIENTS

1 pint of whipped cream
1/2 pound fresh strawberries
1 ripe banana sliced into 3 or 4 long thin strips
Hot fudge sauce
Chopped walnuts
1 Maraschino cherry

You want to whip your cream into a sweet, fluffy mound of delectable taste, and place it in a cool serving bowl (keep the bowl in the freezer until ready for use), along with room temperature bowls for the other ingredients.

Place them all on a serving tray and adjourn to the bedroom (or other choice of den of iniquity), take all your clothes off, and have your partner serve it on your belly, starting just below the navel.

Begin with an even, but thick lathered base of whipped cream, followed by a healthy serving of fresh strawberries on top (if not in season, fresh frozen will also work nicely), then gently sprinkle some nuts over the spread, proceeded by a strategically placed banana strip or two, and topped off with a generous pouring of warm hot fudge sauce (but, like a baby's bath, the temperature must be pleasant to the skin). Kat says that this little belly delight should be approached slowly, from the side, and that the taste should be enjoyed first with the tongue, then with the lips, and ultimately by gentle and tasteful nibblings.

Kat encourages you to stick around, experiment and enjoy the taste. Who knows, you may come up with an equally tempting variation or two on this theme.

TIA'S TIGHTLY PACKED FUDGE

Tia is Irish, with red hair, blue eyes, and a powerfully built anatomy. She also has an incredible recipe for packed fudge. Tia knows chocolate works better than any antidepressant, releasing euphoric-like chemicals into the pleasure center of the brain, which helps stimulate sexual desires. It beats Xanax. She says that if you want to try something that melts in your mouth and not in your hand, try her treat. If you want it to melt someplace else, then stop by and see her at the Stardust Ranch, in Ely, Nevada.

INGREDIENTS
12 ounce Baker's German sweet chocolate, broken into pieces
12 ounces semisweet or bitter sweet morsels
1 (7 ounce) jar marshmallow cream
4 1/2 cups sugar
2 tablespoons of butter
1 (13 ounces) can evaporated milk
1 pinch of salt
2 cups chopped walnuts or pecans

Place the chocolate bars, chocolate morsels and marshmallow cream in the large bowl of an electric mixer.

Combine the sugar, milk, butter, and salt in a 3 quart sauce pan. Bring to a gradual boil over high heat, stirring constantly so nothing burns or adheres to the pot, boiling for exactly 6 minutes, stirring constantly. At the end of 6 minutes, pour over the chocolate mixture, and beat until well blended. Next beat in the vanilla and walnuts.

Finally, pour it all into a buttered 13" x 9" x 2" pan. Let the tightly packed fudge cool at room temperature for 24 hours before cutting it. Cut into 1" squares, which should yield 117 of them (we counted!), then pack in air tight containers. Store what you don't eat right away in a cool but dry place, not in your refrigerator, otherwise the fudge will lose its shine.

CREAMED BANANA WAFERS

*"My girlfriend couldn't make banana cream pie,
but she sure knew how to cream a banana."*

—Attributed to television personality
Soupy Sales in the late 1960s

There's a tall southern lady with short dark hair, brown eyes, soft spoken, with large pouting red lips that are most inviting. She goes by the name of Dallas, and can be seen playing at the Stardust in Ely, Nevada.

She's an expert in having fun, knows a thing or two about bananas, and can highly recommend this creamed treat.

INGREDIENTS

4 ounces of softened butter
6 ounces of fine sugar
3/8 cup genuine maple syrup
3 ounces flour
2 egg whites
1 cup heavy cream
4 small bananas

Mash the butter and sugar together until it's a fluffy consistency and put to one side. In a separate bowl beat your egg whites until they are also white and fluffy. Finally, blend in your genuine maple syrup and flour with the softened butter and sugar, then fold in your fluffy egg whites.

On baking sheets place droplets of the above prepared wafer mixture and then bake at 350 degrees (about 15 minutes or until they are golden brown and thin.) Take out and cool. These will be thin little wafer cookies which will be used to sandwich the creamed banana mixture.

You next want to prepare your creamed banana mixture by gently peeling three of the bananas from the tip to the bottom, placing them in a mashing bowl, and going to work on them, either firmly squeezing them with your hands, or with a fork. In a separate bowl you'll want to whip up the 1 cup of heavy cream until it starts to get firm, at which point you need to add it to the creamed bananas.

This recipe will make about 18 wafers. When you're ready to serve them slice your remaining banana and place the pieces along with your banana cream inside the wafers and enjoy the treat.

"Do you know how to make a pussy talk?
By sticking a tongue in her."

—Attributed to television and movie star
Mamie Van Doren in the 1960s

STORMY NIGHT DELIGHT

Stormy is a black haired, dark eyed, tight bodied girl who parties at the Old Bridge Ranch close to Reno. She's in great shape physically, and knows how to take care of herself when it comes to eating sweets.

She says this recipe is a fresh fruit topping to be served on genuine vanilla ice cream, on hot summer nights, preferably with all your clothes off.

INGREDIENTS

2 cups water
2 cups sugar
6 ripe peaches, pitted and halved (with peels left on)
2 pints strawberries, washed and hulled

In a large enough sauce pan combine your water and sugar, gradually bringing to a boiling point over medium high oven heat. Cook for about 5 minutes, then add the peaches, letting them simmer for about 8-10 minutes, at which point you'll add the strawberries, cooking it all for another 5 minutes. Remove from heat.

Serve 1 peach half, and a scoop full of strawberries (warm), over your balls of vanilla ice cream. Enjoy.

"When the games
are over, the fun begins."

—Stormy

THE PERFECT TART

Briana could easily be classified as the perfect tart. Sharp in character and taste. Hailing from the Kit Kat Ranch in the Golden Triangle just outside Carson City, this sex goddess has a lot going for her, including this recipe.

She says *"The Perfect Tart"* is served flat, like a pizza.

INGREDIENTS

1 roll of Pillsbury sugar cookie dough
6 ounces of cream cheese
2 cups fresh fruit (strawberries, bananas, mangos) sliced
1 jar of orange marmalade
1/3 cup lemon juice (from fresh-squeezed lemons if available)
3/4 cup powdered sugar

Smash and roll your cookie dough into a thin pizza pastry crust shape, then bake it on a cookie tin for 11 to 12 minutes until it's uniformly brown. Remove from oven and let it cool down.

In a bowl you want to next mix the cream cheese and powdered sugar together, then spread it evenly onto the pastry crust.

Finally brush on the marmalade jam, followed by the lemon juice, and top it with your sliced fruit.

Serve anytime you're ready.

*An old spinster whom life
had made mellow,
bought a piece of first-class bordello.
"I am not," she'd impart, "an incipient tart.
I'm just trying to meet the right fellow!"*

A TASTE OF
THE FLAME

Flame is one wild cowgirl with burning auburn hair and a body that's pretty hot too. When not working at P.J.'s Lucky Strike, she can be found riding the rodeo circuit. Her specialty is barrel racing, of which she is prime competition caliber. She says the rodeo circuit has its *"ups and downs, just like a cat house."*

She also says that this treat can be prepared virtually anywhere there's heat, from your kitchen to your campsite or roundup, as no baking in the oven is necessary. But, if you're into *"some fun loving from a different kind of oven"* pay her a visit. She'll get you cooking in no time.

INGREDIENTS

1/4 cup sugar
1/2 cup very strong, hot black coffee
1/4 cup brandy
2 egg yolks, mildly beaten
1 cup whipped cream

Dissolve the sugar in the hot coffee, along with the brandy, then pour it over the egg yolks, stirring it into a nicely blended consistency inside a double boiler over hot water (you don't want it to burn up, so that's why you use the double boiler), until it becomes the consistency of custard.

At this point take the mixture off the heat and let it cool down, then refrigerate it until you're ready to serve. Lop on loads of whip cream at the time of serving and enjoy the results.

"A hard man is good to find."

— Flame

Banana
Lickety Split Combo

"Don't forget the nuts."
— Toni's recommendation

Toni likes to call this treat *"the big stick,"* and she encourages aggressive preparation with basic food groups. She says that if you're into eating more than the basic food groups, come by and see her at the New Sagebrush Red Light Ranch, and she'll be happy to turn you on to other edible items.

INGREDIENTS

1 banana
1 jar of cherry sweetener
A handful of nuts
1 pint of whipped cream
1 pint of strawberries
1 pint of vanilla ice cream

You want to have a platter full of these goodies before you head to the bedroom for a fast and delectable food treat.

Toni says to take strong desire and a willing partner, add a dose of sensuality with a stroke of a hand, a nibble on the ear, a gentle caress, one pint of strawberries, vanilla ice cream with some banana (which you peel with your teeth), and a can of whipped cream (that you proceed to spread all over each other), add a dollop or two of cherry sweetener, and the beginnings are there for a tasty adventure.

Sensually peel the banana, while gently wrapping your hand around it, and begin to lick in an up and down motion. Add some whip cream, and the rest is up to your imagination.

But don't forget the nuts.

BLUE BALLS

Two acres of free land and a mule kick. Ouch and oh my god, the pain. Feeling a little *"testy"* are we? Sometimes the withholding of sexual favors can have extreme physiological consequences on a guy. Black and blue ahi (aha!) takes on a whole new dimension. *"Unspanked tuna"* indeed.

However, when that happens, it's time to gently sit back and enjoy a treat that Alisha from the New Sagebrush Red Light Ranch says will help calm you down, and start to make you feel good all over (again): Sweet Baked Blueberries.

INGREDIENTS

1 quart fresh blueberries
1 tablespoon cinnamon
2 tablespoons lemon juice
1 cup flour
1 cup sugar
1/4 pound butter
1 quart genuine vanilla ice cream

You want to preheat your oven to 350 F., then gently wash your little blueberries before placing them in a large 1.5 quart casserole baking dish. Pamper these small blue nuggets by gently sprinkling the lemon juice and the cinnamon powder on them and carefully place to one side of the counter.

In a bowl sift the flour and sugar together. At this point you want to chop the butter into the mixture until it's crumbling, then sprinkle all of it over your blueberries.

Bake for 45 minutes and serve with vanilla ice cream on top.

STEPHENI'S
SWEET CREAMY TREAT

Stepheni is sweet, and can be earthy and elegant whenever she wants. She's friendly and attractive, and although she doesn't cook in the kitchen that much, she says that she's enjoyed sex there a few times.

She is currently in residence at CharDon's cat house in Elko, which until recently was known as the Mona Lisa. Blonde hair with blue eyes and fair skin, she' a breast-fed baby with a friendly smile.

Her recipe is quick and easy to make, and complements whatever summer berries are in season and available to you. The items you need to obtain in advance are available from the **Williams-Sonoma Catalog** (see the back of the book for reference).

INGREDIENTS

1 pound triple cream cheese
2 cups heavy cream
2 tablespoons Chambord (or other raspberry liqueur)
2 tablespoons lemon juice
1 cup confectioner's sugar
1 cup fruit puree
1 pint fresh strawberries
4 eight-ounce heart-shaped molds (from Williams-Sonoma)

Line your heart-shaped molds with 2 layers of damp cheese cloth and put to one side. In a mixing bowl mix the triple cream cheese, 1/3 cup of cream, Chambord, and lemon juice until smooth. In another bowl blend the remaining cream and sugar until it's a fluffy texture. Combine both bowls and mix together well.

Scoop the cream cheese mixture into the molds, cover with plastic wrap, and refrigerate for 6 hours.

Serve when ready, by unwrapping the molds and decorating each cream delight with fruit puree topped with raspberries.

SPOTTED DICK

*"To be able to fulfill a need of a fellow human being
and profit by it is good business, besides being
an act of faith and sometimes charity."*
—Margo St. James, COYOTE

Sherri is six feet tall, with richly eccentric characteristics. There's not much she probably hasn't done, or wouldn't try at least once, provided it expanded her creative consciousness. She's oral, and likes to talk about it ...with a charm and personality that could easily sway angels or Hell's Angels. And she likes to fly too. So, if you're interested in joining "the mile high club" she encourages you to stop by for a visit with her at the Stardust Ranch in Ely "to fly the friendly thighs united."

For a culinary treat that won't jerk you around, Sherri suggests a little "Spotted Dick."

INGREDIENTS

4 ripe bananas, peeled and sliced diagonally
1 cup heavy cream
2 tablespoons unsalted butter
3 tablespoons brandy
1/4 teaspoon salt
1/4 cup sugar
1/4 teaspoon nutmeg
5 ounces white chocolate (coarsely grated)
5 ounces dark semi sweet chocolate (coarsely grated)

Combine the cream, butter, brandy, salt, sugar, and nutmeg in a saucepan over medium heat on your oven, and gradually bring to a boil, at which point you'll want to reduce the heat and simmer for about 5 minutes, allowing the mixture to thicken (enough to coat the back of a spoon).

Add the banana slices next, and warm them for about 1 minute. Remove and serve on dessert plates with the coarse chocolate sprinkled over them.

FALLEN ANGEL HAIR PIE

Traci out at the Stardust in Ely has a great recipe for pie. More than just edible hair pie in your face. Delightful little curly cues, sweet tasting stuff that's as American as peaches and cream. Blonde hair, blue eyes, suggestive pouting lips, with an attitude that suggests all-American fun . . . and games.

Traci is a wonderful athlete, be it tennis, golf or billiards. As you might be able to tell, her talents involve moving balls from point A to point B. She's a temptress as well as instructress. If you have a favorite game in mind involving balls, look her up. She invites you. She challenges you.

Her peach cobbler dessert is equally inviting.

INGREDIENTS

3 cups sliced fresh or canned peaches
1 tablespoon lemon juice
1 cup flour
1/2 teaspoon salt
1 beaten egg
6 tablespoons butter, melted

Place your sliced peaches in the bottom of a 10 x 6 x 2 inch baking dish and sprinkle them with lemon juice.

Next, in a mixing bowl, sift together your other ingredients, then toss in the egg, mixing well until the ingredients become crumbly, at which point you want to spread that over the peaches. Finally, drizzle your melted butter over the top.

Bake at 375 degrees for 35-40 minutes until done.

Traci says that as a variation you can peel the peaches and when the cobbler is 5 minutes from done, add back the peach peels and they'll look like *"little curly whirlies"* when cooked, giving you the *"hair pie look."*

Sarah Lee Box Cake with Hard Nut Frosting

Sarah Lee works in a cat house in Elko called Mona's. Located on South 3rd Street just past the railroad tracks, in a building that's as old as the town itself. And if the walls could talk, many a fine book on sex therapy could be written.

Sarah Lee considers herself to be a sex therapist in residence. Mind you, not "like a sex therapist." As she states, *the only 'like' about it is what the customer will like about it!"* She's an expert in Sex 101, and encourages all aspiring students to pay her a visit for her next class and demonstration.

She also encourages you to try her box cake with hard nut frosting.

INGREDIENTS

2 cups flour
2 teaspoons baking powder
1/2 teaspoon baking soda
Dash of salt
5/8 cup cocoa
1.5 cups sugar
5/8 cup vegetable shortening
1/2 cup water
2/3 cup milk
2 eggs
1 teaspoon vanilla extract

In a bowl you're going to mix all of the above mentioned ingredients, until it reaches a smooth consistency (about 4 minutes with your mixing blender, or a few minutes longer if you whip this stuff by hand).

When it's ready to pour out, do so in a sheet cake pan, or use two 9-inch layer cake pans and bake 25-30 minutes (until the proverbial toothpick comes clean, or when you pat the center of the cake with your fingers it rebounds right back). Let it cool down before removing from the pan. Sarah Lee says *"box cake should be served moist."*

INGREDIENTS FOR HARD NUT FROSTING:

9 egg yolks
1.5 cups sugar
1.6 cups evaporated milk
2 cups chopped walnuts

In a sauce pan, caressingly blend the first three ingredients before adding the nuts, then cook over moderate heat until it bubbles and thickens. At this point it's done, so cool it down before applying to the cake.

If you try spreading this over each other, you can bet that more than just nuts will be hard.

LIGHTLY DUSTED BALLS

Walk into the Old Bridge Ranch and you'll immediately feel comfortable and welcome, courtesy of the nice ladies working there. Whether you're there to exchange "oral pleasantries" or have them demonstrate their myriad skills, many of these courtesans could blow your mind (and perhaps something else too, along the way).

Madison happens to be one of them. Alabaster complexion, cornflower eyes and an extravagant mass of beautiful blonde hair match up well with her other attributes, including her outgoing personality.

Madison has seen some balls in her time. Possibly everything from white multispeed vibratones and "Thelma's Grapes," to chocolate covered ones on a big stick (see references for **Plain Wrapped Chocolates**).

Her recipe for "Lightly Dusted Balls" involves the cookie dough kind.

INGREDIENTS

2 cubes of butter
6 tablespoons sugar
2 cups flour
1 teaspoon vanilla extract
3/4 cup chopped walnuts
2 tablespoons Amaretto liqueur

Preheat your oven to 350 degrees F. Mix all your ingredients together well, then gently shape your dough into little orbs about 1.5 inches in diameter.

Madison says to place the balls on cookie sheets and bake for about 10-12 minutes or until they're slightly brown on the bottoms. Remove from oven, and when cooled down, roll the little nuggets in powdered sugar and serve naked with a big wet kiss.

Aroma
Therapy

APHRODISIACS, FOOD & THERAPY

*"Let food be your medicine
and medicine be your food."*

—— Hippocrates

The foods you eat can make major health and performance differences on your mind and body. We're talking cerebral excitation, antiseptic properties, antimicrobial abilities, along with an overall improvement of sexual functions and capabilities.

What we have culled here from covens, ancient hieroglyphics, old wive's tales, superstitions and observations of wildly primitive tribes is presented forthwith. Some of it may actually work, it's all been written about before, and it's probably available for further perusal from many libraries and bookstores, perhaps in your community.

A few of the more basic possibilities include:

Cranberries and cranberry juice. They appear to have possible therapeutic benefits. Folklore touts them as preventatives for urinary tract and bladder infections. The theory here is that the cranberry juice survives digestion and ends up in urine, where it prevents bacteria from adhering to cells in the urinary tract. Take note though, it does not work for everyone, and it's not supposed to be a substitute for antibiotic drugs.

Peas. Plain old green ones. Some people think that peas interfere with the reproductive hormones progesterone and estrogen, and reduce sperm counts, making pregnancy less likely. But don't hold your breath in anticipation of having the Jolly Green Giant save you on this. Practice safe sex with your "jolly giant," and think about what you're doing before you become a goober yourself.

Ginseng. This comes from the Chinese "jen shen," which means "man root." Used for its tonic and aphrodisiac properties, enhancing sexual lust and desire. The Chinese realized 2,000 years ago that ginseng increased longevity. Anything that looks like a "man's root," and causes longevity sounds good to me.

Oysters. They resemble human testes and apparently have an effect on them as well. Oysters are rich in zinc, which is essential for the production of the male hormone testosterone. It's simple: No zinc, you shrink!

Celery and pineapple juice. They contain high concentrations of aspartic acid and the amino acid phenylalanine, and reportedly can change the taste of semen from something unpalatable to that of an aromatic fruit cocktail.

There are also several legal prosexual drugs and nutrients out there which can improve sex and sexual health, helping to enhance sexual drive, erections, the intensity of orgasms, while overcoming impotence, premature ejaculation, nocturnal emissions, and several other pronounced sexual difficulties. These include vitamin supplements, acupuncture and the telling of erotic bedtime stories to you by naughty, naked story tellers.

Check it all out, have an open mind, and remember, the most powerful aphrodisiac in the world is contained between your ears.

Appendix

GLOSSARY OF TERMS
CATALOGS & REFERENCES
ORDER FORM

GLOSSARY
OF TERMS

—A FEW GOODIES FROM A to Z—

Alka Seltzer: Sexual act involving the use of alka seltzer, and performed by women by inserting a moistened piece of it inside her at the time of climax, intended to create a fizzy finish and help alleviate the guy's headache.

Ambergris: An aphrodisiac thought to be formed by the feces of the sperm whale impacted around a core of solid matter, such as giant squid beaks.

Aphrodisiacs: Sexual stimulants (such as the horn of rhino, erect penis of horse, ambergris, smoked hump of camel and chocolate).

Arm & Hammer Baking Soda: Removes all body odor when applied to the body.

Aroma Therapy: Pure essential oils, either inhaled or applied to the skin, including rose oil, jasmine and sandalwood.

Around the World: The reaming of the buttock and rectum with one's tongue (after applying Arm & Hammer Baking Soda to it).

Binaca Blast: Oral sex by a woman with her mouth full of Binaca, cool and refreshing.

Booga Booga: Term used to describe the sexual act in primitive societies.

Box Lunch: Served in many of the cat houses, along with a side of thighs.

Brothel Sprout: Term used to describe a working girl who has burned out, going past the *al dente* stage into the crisp fried, burnt out mode of existence.

Cardamom: A spice that's a member of the ginger family; its oil is known as the *"Fire of Venus."* It helps to mask bad odors and bad breath.

Casa Roll: Term used to describe sex with an Hispanic person.

Crudites: Raw vegetables cut into pieces and served with dip as an appeteaser. Outrageous sex acts that take place in some of the brothels.

Cum Tu Soon: Faster than a New York minute.

Dicteria: Greek house of prostitution (around 500 B.C.).

Edible Undies: Flavor fresh garments that dissolve in water or excessive moisture. Ideal for quickie lunches, snacks, or as an *hors d'oeuvre.*

Fetishists: Individuals whose sexual interests are concentrated exclusively on certain body parts, or on certain portions of the attire.

Ginger: Tropical herb (dried root) grown in the East Indies, and used as an aphrodisiac in China for 3,000 years. What Fred Astaire's nose smelled like.

Goo In Hand: Coming to dinner alone, or *"menage a uno."*

Gumbo: A thick stew made with fish or fowl, and served on a bed of white rice. What John Derek might like to do at night after he takes his teeth out.

Hedonism: The doctrine or philosophy of belief that pleasure or happiness is the sole or chief goal in life.

Hookers: Named in honor of Joseph Hooker (1814-1879), *"Fighting Joe"* Brigadier General during the Civil War, known for restoring the Union Army's combat spirit by supplying his troops with *"charity ladies,"* who became known as *"Hookers."* He died on Halloween.

Kaiser Roll: Sex with a German.

Limp Noodle: What happens to a guy's love club when he drinks too much at a cat house and stays in a hot tub too long with the girl of his dreams.

Meat Loaf: Something a virile guy should never let happen to his. As one great hooker said, *"Don't ever let your meat loaf."*

Nay Nays: Milk cans, bazooms, fun bags, num nums, moo moos, twin doves, high beams, snowy hillocks, melons, teats, snuggle-pups.

Olive Oil: A cooking oil pressed from ripe olives. What Popeye would place his tumescent love log into when lustful desires overcame him.

Onanism: The practice of becoming intimate with oneself. Also known as *"menage a uno,"* and *"menage a lefty."*

Pearl Necklace: Sexual activity involving the man placing his tumescent love club between a woman's breasts, then rocking gently back and forth, culminating in the ejaculation of his pearl drops love beads around her neck from his wank wank sack bag.

Priapism: Suffering from a continuous hard on.

Priapus: Ancient Greek god who suffered from a continuous stiffy.

Puff Pastry: A morning treat with a nice working girl.

Pu Yi: Inedible panties. Clothes pins extra.

Sauer Kraut: Term used to describe sex with a German who hasn't bathed lately.

Spotted Dick: A tasty dessert, but something you wouldn't want to wake up to in the morning.

Suc Mi Wang: Non-traditional oriental meatloaf.

Testaclees: Erroneously considered to be a Greek sexual god who was big into nuts, not to be confused with Priapus, the mythological god who had a persistent erection.

Two Can Chew: Oriental sixty-nine.

Turnover: A breakfast dessert from a different position.

Wai Tu Yung: Not available on school nights.

Wind, Rain & Lava: Sex act involving being blown (or farted on), then pissed on, then finally shat upon with excreta.

Won Hung Lo: Disproportionate oriental meatballs.

CATALOGS
& REFERENCES

1. *Plain Wrapped Chocolates* (for adults). This company has sexually representative erotic chocolate shapes and colors for every part of the anatomy. These chocolates are hand poured and make great gifts. They can be reached in Georgetown, Texas, at 512/930-9793, Fax 512/819-9320. Their Web Site on the Internet shows you more of what they offer. The address is: http://www.eden.com/~plainwrp/choco/. Their e-mail address is: chocolate@plainwrap.com

2. *The Stamford Collection Catalog.* This company has been in business since 1969, and they have hundreds of exciting products, including *"Kiss of Mint"* condoms, Dr. Cassidy's Medical Extensions (add extra inches with this soft and pliable latex roll-on), lubricants, stimulators and titilizers. They can be reached at 718/389-6433 for customer service.

3. *Intimate Treasures Catalog.* They call themselves the "catalog of catalogs," and offer dozens of other adult catalogs, from main stream adult couples to fantasy, exotic, bizarre, fetish, and wild. Their address is Box 77902, San Francisco, CA 94107-0902. They can be reached at 415/863-5002 for customer service.

4. *The Perfect Condom.* They are America's first condom store with a Web Site (http://www.condomania.com). This heavily hit Web Site has lots of goodies and information, and proclaim themselves to be the gurus of safer sex, with answers, advice, etc. If you have a question about thinner, stronger, or safer contact them. 800/9CONDOM. Their e-mail address is: informl@condomania.com

5. *Dream Dresser Catalog.* Box 16158, Beverly Hills, CA 90209-2158. This company has some of the finest leather and latex sexual attire and accoutrements if you're into *"nasty"* and custom built. With retail outlets in Georgetown, Washington, DC (1042 Wisconsin Ave.), 202/625-0373, and in West Hollywood, CA (8444-50 Santa Monica Blvd.), 213/848-3480. The price of the full color catalog is $10, and worth it. For mail order call 213/848-3480.

6. *Champagne Fashions Catalog.* They have one of the most extensive collections of superior quality leather and PVC vinyl fashions currently available anywhere, for women. Located at Box 4945 Toms River, NJ 08754-4945. 800/244-3108.

7. *Raven Hill Studios.* Adult spanking films, where *"black and blue"* has nothing to do with tuna. Located at Box 67062, St. Petersburg, FL 33736. 813/363-7501. Fax 813/367-1967.

8. *Fredericks of Hollywood Catalog.* Great models in terrific clothes for virtually every scenario you'd ever want to play out.

9. *Centurians Leather Catalog.* The largest fetish supplier in the world, including "Bondage in a Box." This is not exactly your typical Tupper Ware Party, but a peek at their catalog might give you some ideas to pursue. They have over 20,000 bizarre items available. 714/971-9877.

10. *Victoria's Secret Catalog.* More beautiful models wearing virtually nothing to everything. They can be reached at Box 16589, Columbus, OH 43216. Customer Service: 800/888-1500.

11. *Fantasy Island Catalog.* The ultimate in adult playroom accessories, from toys to tools, over 50 pages of possibilities.

12. *PENet.* (http://www.creative.net/~penet/). This is for Prostitutes Education Network. If you want statistics and information about prostitution issues, this is a good place to start.

13. *COYOTE ("Call Off Your Old Tired Ethics")* was founded by Margo St. James in 1973, and works for the rights of all sex workers: strippers, phone operators, prostitutes, porn actresses, etc. It supports programs to assist sex workers in their choice to change their occupation, and to educate sex workers, their clients, and the general public about safe sex. They can be reached at 415/435-7950 in San Francisco, and 818/892-1859 in Los Angeles.

14. *The Good Looks Company Catalog.* Your source for the adult novelty gift market. 800/666-3531. Located at 2762 S. La Cienega Blvd., Los Angeles, CA 90039. Everything from penis pasta and pasta boobs to the dancing banana and anatomy ties, this catalog has lots of fun gag gift items worth checking out.

15. *Fantasy Library Catalog.* Some of the best publications available, along with rare and unusual erotica from around the world. Can be reached at 415/435-7950 in San Francisco, and 818/892-1859 in Los Angeles.

16. *Mind Candy Emporium Catalog.* For discriminating adults only. From books on the art of spanking, to compendiums on nudism, there's lots to read here. Located at Box 931437, Cherokee Avenue, Hollywood, CA 90093. 818/886-1714. Fax 818/886-0017.

17. *Playboy Catalog.* If you've seen their magazine, this is pretty much an order form from it. Lots of good stuff here from clothes to books, videos and fun accessories. 800/423-9494.

18. *Bizarre Publishing.* This magazine is dedicated to the most erotic organ in the human body: the human mind! True life fetish adventures, leather and latex fashion news, cross dressing, etc. Located at Box 429, Orange, CA 92666.

19. *The Erotic Bakery.* They'll bake up whatever you want, in whatever shape or size, and ship it to you UPS. Located on 45th Avenue in Seattle, WA.

20. *Edible Undies.* These are novelty items good for snacks, quickie lunches, Sunday brunch, or great as hors d'oeuvres. Guaranteed flavor fresh. From Kingman Industries, Murrieta, CA 92562.

ORDER FORM

If you want to know more about legal prostitution in Nevada, please order *THE OFFICIAL GUIDE TO THE BEST CAT HOUSES IN NEVADA, Everything You Want to Know About Legal Prostitution,* by J.R. Schwartz, for $14.95. Each order is personally signed in bold red felt tip ink by the author, J.R. Schwartz, and comes with one pack of souvenir cat house matches, and one sex pleasure menu from the wildest cat houses in Nevada!

BY HOOK OR BY COOK, THE OFFICIAL CAT HOUSE COOK BOOK, edited by J.R. Schwartz, for $14.95. Each order is personally signed by J.R. Schwartz, and comes with one pack of souvenir cat house matches, and one sex pleasure menu from the wildest cat houses in Nevada.

J.R., PLEASE SEND ME THE FOLLOWING:

_____ *The Official Guide to the Best Cat Houses in Nevada,* along with one sex pleasure menu and one pack of cat house matches, for $14.95.

_____ *By Hook or By Cook, The Official Cat House Cookbook,* along with one sex pleasure menu and one pack of cat house matches, for $12.95.

_____ *Send me both!* I want *The Official Guide to the Best Cat Houses in Nevada,* and *By Hook or By Cook, The Official Cat House Cook Book,* along with two sex pleasure menus and two packs of cat house matches, for only $20.00 (that's a savings of $7.90).

Enclose $3.00 additional per book to cover postage and handling (and Idaho residents please add 5% sales tax).

I understand that I may return any and all items for a complete refund of my money if for any reason I'm not satisfied.

MAIL TO:
J.R. SCHWARTZ
Box 1810
Boise, Idaho 83701-1810
Visit my Web Site for more fun stuff:
http://www.hookers.com/
or e-mail me at: hooker1@micron.net

The research J.R. SCHWARTZ did on his previous best-seller, *The Official Guide to the Best Cat Houses in Nevada,* worked up his appetite for more information on the *second* oldest profession, cooking.

By Hook or By Cook goes where no cookbook has dared to go, and if laughter is the best thing for our digestion, J.R.'s latest book is the answer.

The author lives with his bird "Cosmo," in Boise, Idaho, and has appeared on *CNN Nightly News* and several other national TV and radio programs.